Y0-BZL-408

Contents

Editor's Note

SAMUEL DICKEY GORDON (1859-1936) was a popular Christian lecturer, whose famous "Quiet Talks" series inspired many people to walk more closely with Christ. Dickey spent eleven years as a leader in the Y.M.C.A. in Pennsylvania and Ohio. Then in 1895 he embarked on his service of Christian teaching, which at one point took him on a four-year tour of Europe and the Orient.

Between 1901 and 1936, Gordon published twenty-five books in his "Quiet Talks" series. The best known among these is *Quiet Talks on Prayer*, which is a Christian classic. Since it appeared in 1904, that little book has helped many of us learn how to converse with God reverently and effectively.

Gordon possessed an understanding of Christian living which was grounded in biblical and practical wisdom. His depth and simplicity still speak to us, despite the enormous social and material changes which have occurred since he wrote.

Quiet Talks on the Healing Christ, now *The Healing Christ*, first appeared in 1924. In this book, Gordon offers a brief, yet thorough picture of healing and health in God's plan. He studies

God's mind about healing by looking at "the Book of God" and "the Book of Life," illuminating scripture from experience, and vice versa.

This present volume has been updated for modern readers. Some passages were excised which were based on conclusions which modern medical science has altered. These are corrections which Gordon himself would have welcomed. For the most part, however, the inspiring truths of these "Quiet Talks" stand as Gordon wrote them.

Preface

CHRIST WILL EAGERLY MEET every need of a person's life to the full. If we don't have all we need, the trouble isn't with the hand that gives but the hand that takes. No man's hand has ever reached up to take as much as the pierced hand is reaching down to give. But giving without hurting is a fine art. And the taking needs skill, too, though the simplest may take all he needs. Skill in taking is chiefly skill of the heart.

Teaching is rare. Matured, rounded-out teaching is yet more rare. And the chief need today, in the bustle of daily Christian living is teaching—simple, clear, full, poised teaching.

Healing is a tangled subject. Two others keep it close company, as far as being tangled is concerned, namely, holiness and the return of Christ. It is easy to get warped, unmatured, partial statements on these subjects.

The direct preparation of this book has taken eleven years, the indirect runs further back. I didn't set out to write a book. I felt the need to get my own feet planted firmly on the pavement. I read and watched and prayed to understand for myself. And now I'm giving the substance of my understanding to others, with a prayer that it may help them as it has helped me.

Two books have been constantly studied, the Book of God, and the Book of Life. These two go together. The Book of God is written out of life, under the Holy Spirit's touch and control. The Book of Life is still being written. It takes a simple practice of habitual reading to understand the first. It takes a careful, trained reading habit to read and understand the second.

The Book of God is the teaching book, written out of human experience, and full of illustrations of life. The Book of Life is the illustration book. It contains countless illustrations of all the teachings of the other book. One ought to read both. They fit together, and the conditions for understanding both are the same: a bent will, an open mind, a prayerful spirit, a keenly observing eye, and constant practiced reading. Through this we are able to discern our Father's purposes and plans, *and* how they affect us personally.

So, after these years of study, this book is sent out in Christ's name. And the one conscious purpose is that it may help some to reach up and *take* all the pierced hand is now reaching down to *give*.

Some Principles of Healing Taught in God's Word, Directly and Indirectly

1. It is God's first will that people be pure in heart, clear in mind, strong in purpose, gentle and content in spirit, poised in judgment, happy in circumstances, and strong and well in body.

2. God does not send disease. It comes through some disobedience of the natural laws of the body, conscious or unconscious, though rarely traceable in full. It may come from the Devil, *or* because of the break of sin affecting all life. But it comes *always through* that open door of disobedience to the laws of the body.

3. Christ heals human bodies today by his own direct supernatural touch, sometimes through the physician and the use of medicine, sometimes without medicine, sometimes when medicine is confessedly powerless, and sometimes overcoming the unwise use of medicine. The Holy Spirit's leading is the touchstone.

4. In healing, Christ is always reaching in for the far greater thing, the healing of the spirit, the life.

5. There is sometimes a waiting time, after the conditions are met, before the full healing comes.

There is a disciplinary side in bodily suffering, but the healing comes as quickly as the lesson is learned.

6. The Devil heals human bodies, within sharply defined limits, under disguise, that he may get and tighten his hold on man. He bitterly opposes healing through Christ's supernatural touch. This is particularly true regarding those that have the gift of leadership.

7. The conditions for Christ's healing are the same as for being saved. Trust him fully as your Savior and Master. Then go to him for whatever you need, always seeking the Holy Spirit's guidance.

ONE

The Christ Healing

It is God's first will for every person, everywhere to be pure in heart, straight in life, strong in purpose, clear and open in mind, well-balanced in judgment, gentle in contact with others, at peace within, happy in circumstances, and strong and well in body.

Humanly Impossible

Christ did impossible things, when he was on earth. That is, they were impossible for others. He did them. They were things that needed to be done. Men were helped by them. He eased suffering and more. It took power to do them. It took a power more than the natural power people were familiar with. Others didn't do them because they lacked the power. Christ had the power needed to do the impossible.

Christ taught. He is commonly accepted as mankind's greatest teacher. He also lived what he taught, before he taught it. There was always a reserve of teaching, actually lived, behind each teaching he gave. But Christ did more than teach. He *did* things.

Christ had ideals that far exceeded the ideals of all others. And he attained his ideals in the life he lived. Men saw and felt and experienced things through his touch, things they badly needed but didn't have till he gave them.

The distinctive thing about Christ, of course, is that he died. He died as none other did, nor could, nor can. The most outstanding thing about his life is the end of it. The knot on the end of the thread of his life, that gathered it all up in one, is his death.

But apart from that, the outstanding thing is that Christ did impossible things. Men admire and worship the man who can do outstanding things, actually bring them to pass. Christ did outstanding things.

He fed the hungry thousands with a few scanty loaves. He stilled that sudden Galilean storm that blanched the bronzed cheeks of those hardened sailors, stilled it with a word; and stilled it into a great calm. He helped Peter pay his taxes, in a very unusual way. That sounds very practical today. He robbed the ever-yawning grave of its hopeless victims.

Of all the things Christ did, one stands out. He healed men's bodies of sickness and disease. The world was sick when Christ was here. There was no science of bodily healing. There was natural healing. The Jews have been famous through the centuries for their rare skill in healing through simple remedies. But, characteristically, dominantly, the people were sick. Christ healed men's bodies.

This is what first drew the crowds in notable numbers. That fact itself tells how acute the problem of physical illness was. The need was so great, and so general, that once the word went out, it spread throughout Palestine. The crowds came from everywhere, and they came crowding so thick that they seriously affected his movements.

Hopeless Incurables

History records thirty-three miracles done by Christ. Twenty-eight of them have to do with the body. Twenty-four of them were miracles of healing (including now the three cases of death). Four others have to do with supplying bodily needs.

Sixteen summaries are given of his various activities, including bodily healing. If one looks over these summaries, it becomes clear that the total of those healed probably ran into some several thousands. People came in throngs. They came from all the surrounding countries, from as far away as Tyre.

The four Gospels cite twenty-four individual instances of healing. These become of interest for what they tell of Christ's healing ministry. Of the twenty-four, two could be classified as acute cases. The other twenty-two are all chronic cases, incurables, extreme hopeless incorrigibles. Six (possibly eight) were demon-possessed, reckoned incurable. Three were actually dead. The thirteen others were hopeless incurables.

Christ's healing power extended to the last degree of human need. The humanly impossible yielded to Christ's touch every time. No need was too grave for his healing touch. The Gospel is explicit on this point. The list of diseases specifically named includes epilepsy, dropsy, deafness and dumbness, palsy or paralysis, chronic hemorrhage, demon-possession, leprosy, withered hand (i.e., paralysis), blindness, restoration of an ear that had been cut off, and even death.

One outstanding passage touches the extreme need which Christ's healing covered. Matthew says, "There came unto Him great multitudes, having with them the lame, blind, dumb, *maimed*, and many others, and cast them down at His feet; and He healed them" (Mt 15:30). This is a significant passage. It was clearly an unusual crowd of helpless incurables, brought by their kinsfolk and friends and neighbors. What a sight!

That word "maimed" catches one's eye. It occurs twice. Underneath, the word has two meanings; *crooked* is one, and *mutilated* the other. Its use in Mark 9:43 clearly means a missing limb.

The word for "lame" here is also used in the Mark passage for a severed limb. Christ's healing went to the extent of restoring a lost portion of the body, a limb or an arm or some other part. There were no exceptions so far as need went.

A Great Power at Work

The extent of Christ's power to heal is put in as sweeping language. His power always fully covered the need, whatever that happened to be. There was simply no limit. His healing met every need, and met it fully. It could not have been greater. Three words can be used to describe it. Christ healed *instantly, perfectly,* and *permanently.*

The Gospels recount only one exception. Once, when Christ healed a blind man, the healing went through two stages. First the man saw men "as trees walking," then "all things clearly." The interval of time involved was plainly so brief that it is likely the man himself would have gladly used the word "instantly."

Again that outstanding passage comes in. Its language could not be more graphic and adequate, and yet simple and brief. Matthew says, "The multitudes wondered when they saw the dumb speaking, the maimed whole, and the lame walking, and the blind seeing" (Mt 15:31).

The extent of the power at work is as striking as the sweep of disease covered. There's an overflowing abundance of power. The crowds learned that if they would "only touch the border of his garment," they would know the healing power in their body.

It says "power came forth from him," as though it breathed out of his very presence. The ease of action, and the frequency and extent of Christ's healing power stand in striking contrast to the Old Testament miracles.

The effect on the crowd itself revealed the touch of God. "They *glorified*" God. Exuberant songs of praise were lifted to God. Even the curious crowds that came seeking sensation went away with a hush in their hearts and praises to God on their lips.

It is striking to note that Christ gave this power to his disciples, unschooled and undisciplined as they were, yet devoted to him. Repeatedly they were sent out into the villages and country districts. And they returned with ringing voices and shining faces, telling of the power that had attended their activity. Special emphasis was laid on healing, and on the casting out of evil spirits.

Why Did Christ Heal?

Why did Christ heal? It is never intimated that he did it to let people know that he could. He never used power simply to let men see he had it. It is never suggested that he did mighty works to prove who he was. Incidentally it is made clear that he did have the exceptional power, and that he was the Son of God in the distinctive sense that was true of no other.

Even when John, in the dark of the prison cell, puzzled to know why Christ didn't fill out the official side of the Messiah's task, as well as the personal side, Christ simply pointed out that his works were evidence that the old prophetic picture was being lived out. He comforted John, the lonely prisoner, with the word that John had been true and that there was a waiting time ahead for both of them.

Christ healed people because he couldn't help it. Their need tugged desperately at his heart. He healed people because they needed healing. This stands out first and foremost.

It is true, broadly, as a principle, that miracles came into action throughout scripture to meet some emergency. But, when it comes to the immediate reason why Christ healed, as the narrative runs, it was to meet the personal needs of suffering men and women.

A strong, tender word is constantly on Christ's lips, and spoken about him, "compassion." It means to have the heart tenderly drawn out by need. It really means to suffer in heart because of the suffering of others.

This gives the "why" of Christ's healing. One key-passage may be given as an index to the others, "He had compasison on them, *and* healed their sick." (Mt 14:14. See also 15:32, 20:34, 9:36 with 10:1, Mk 1:41, 6:34, 8:2, Lk 7:13-15.).

He healed because he couldn't help it. He *could* heal, and he couldn't help healing, with such suffering before his eyes. His heart forced him to answer such needs. Healing is a window into Christ's heart. And Christ himself is the open window into the Father's heart.

One afternoon a gentle-faced woman came to me at the close of a meeting and asked abruptly, "Does God answer prayer?" She had a thoughtful face, and looked well cared for.

I didn't say yes. A mere yes seemed too tame with that tense face, and those suffering eyes. I merely said, "Sit down a moment."

With a bit of prayer for guidance, I said, "Has he ever answered a prayer for you, just once?" (For, you remember, one fact establishes a law of action.)

Instantly a startled look came into her eyes. In a low, hushed voice she said, "Oh! I forgot." Then she told in a few words of when her daughter, years before, a child of ten or so then, had been critically ill. The physician had said that the surgery was necessary.

The mother's heart drew back from the thought of having a surgeon's knife cut into that precious little body. Could she have a little time to think about it, she had asked. Yes, there was no immediate pressure, came the reply.

That night she had retired for sleep. She spent much more time than usual on her knees. She didn't ask for healing. She had not been taught that she might.

She simply poured out her heart. God was a good father. The thought of surgery troubled her deeply. A cry rose out of her heart, a yearning cry, inarticulate as to the how. Then she slept quietly.

The morning came, and with it the physician. After the examination a puzzled look came into his eyes. He said quietly, "I don't understand this; but a distinct change has come in your daughter's condition. I won't need to operate. She will get well without the surgery." And she did.

The woman said with a changed voice, "I forgot." Her own experience answered her tense question.

Christ has not changed. His power is at our fingertips now. No need must go unsupplied, if he may have his way.

TWO

Is It Christ's Will to Heal Us Today?

It is God's first will that we should be pure in heart, gripped by a nobly strong purpose, balanced in our understanding of things, humanly gentle in our personal contacts, at sweet peace within, content in circumstances, and healthy and hearty in our bodies.

The World Is Sick

Is it Christ's will to heal our bodies of sickness and disease and weakness today? He can, of course. He has the power. Is he willing to do it? Does he think it wise to? Is it part of his plan for us at the present time?

There is need enough surely. Oh! there is more health than disease, more strength than weakness, more life than death. This is true. Yet the race is sick and diseased.

There is a modern science of bodily healing today that was nonexistent a century ago. It is a real science, based on knowledge of the human body, substances found in nature, of substances

11

created in the laboratory, and of their action on the body. It is based upon a vast accumulation of experience, and of skill. It is a rare combination of science and of art, acquired skill in action.

There is also an unhelpful professional pride in the medical profession, as in all professional circles. The effect of this pride is to move the profession toward commercialism. And there is confessedly a vast amount of guesswork and of experimenting, at human expense of pain and suffering, and worse. Yet the fact stands out that we have a science of bodily healing. And its success in healing and relieving suffering through the years is clear beyond words to describe or imagination to picture.

It is a striking fact that some of the most prominent leaders in medicine support a movement away from drugs and surgery, and toward advice about the intelligent care of the body. This is called preventive medicine.

A long list of quotations could be given from the most eminent physicians around the world against the use of drugs and concerning the injuries inflicted by guesswork and experiment. These quotations magnify the place of nature in healing, through means, aside from remedies, and often overcoming the drugs given.

Doctors emphasize intelligence in the selection of foods, a wise obedience to bodily laws, and the distinct bearing of the mental and spiritual mood and attitude on bodily conditions.

It should be noted also that, quite apart from any direct action on God's part, one's mental attitude has incalculable influence on the body. It greatly affects the bodily conditions at all times, and in disease and times of crisis it is often apt to be the decisive factor.

Modern medicine recognizes that stress and fear alter the normal balance of the body, opening the door for certain kinds of disease. A simple heart-trust in God and his goodness, with the confidence that accompanies it, actually creates a healthier body. I am not speaking now of the numerous imaginary ills, but of actual physical conditions.

Yet, notwithstanding the science of healing, the fact remains that at every corner, pathetically, tragically, the world is sick, bodily ill. Is it God's will to heal our bodies today? There's surely need enough. He *can* do it but will he? Does he want to? Is it in his heart and purpose to do it?

It is God's first will for every man that he shall be pure in heart, strong and noble in purpose, gentle in human contact, happy in circumstances, at peace in his inner spirit, and strong and well in body.

A Blessed Healing Trail

The Bible gives us a clear view of God's attitude toward healing. It is striking to find out how the other book, the Book of Life (or experience), tallies up with, and illustrates this written book, as of course it would. For the Bible is a part of the Book of Life. It grew up out of human life. These are our two chief books of study.

It is striking to look at life as it was in the garden of Eden. For that was life as God intended it. There, Adam and Eve lived in perfect health of body and spirit, in a happy, unbroken relationship. They had fullness of life, perfect health. Such things as weakness, disease, or death were unknown.

The Book of Job may be one of the oldest books of the Bible. It is devoted to the sorest question of human life, that is, human suffering, *and* God's solution. We usually miss that *and*.

The Book of Job contains two parts: Job's suffering, and the outcome. We have been fed with stories about the first part, the suffering. The second part, the outcome, has been strangely ignored. Yet it is the bigger part.

Job suffers indeed, in family, in circumstances, and then in body. Then the healing touch comes, and all is changed. Even the ash-heap he sits in becomes fragrant, for it was the gateway to a new life of the spirit, and so to bodily health and vigor, and all else that came. As the gateway of God's Book, Job's story offers this stirring message: it is God's will to heal the inner heart and life, *and* the body.

Note that the theme of healing runs unbroken through the Bible. The teaching trail and the healing trail persist throughout side by side. It is a threefold healing—protection from actual disease just at hand, the continuance of health and vigor through the unseen touch of God, and the physical healing of bodily disease.

The theme runs from Eve's recognition that it was through that touch on her body that weakness was overcome (and she was able to go through what has become the severest bodily test of life [Gn 4:1 with 3:16]), on through Abimelech's experience (Gn 20:17-18), and Sarah's (Gn 21:1-2, 11:30, and 17:16, 17), Rebekah's (Gn 25:21) and Rachel's (Gn 29:31, 30:22-24), Moses' leprous hand (Ex 4:6-7), and Miriam's leprous body (Nm 12:9-15).

The remarkable experience of freeing of the Hebrew people from the Egyptians reveals the unseen touch of God, giving unusual bodily vigor under sore physical stress, and protecting from disease.

There's an outstanding account at the beginning of the training of the new messenger nation. Israel was to become the world's teacher-nation. As they enter their long session of schooling, special emphasis is laid on God's eager willingness to heal.

It comes first in the flush of the tremendous Red Sea deliverance, when they were peculiarly sensitive to impressions. In the tense plea that they keep in full touch with their Deliverer comes this: "I will put none of the diseases upon thee which I have put upon the Egyptians; for I am the Lord that healeth thee" (Ex 15:26).

God extended the triple healing: protection from, the touch of continuous health, and the actual physical healing. Then under the hush and awe of the lone mountain, all aflame with the presence of their wondrous God, in the midst of a yearning plea to them to keep in touch with him, this word rings out: "I will take sickness away from the midst of thee. There shall none cast her young, nor be barren in thy land: the number of thy days I will fullfil" (Ex 23:25-26).

So the trail persists. Solomon remembers it in the great temple prayer (1 Kg 8:37-38). It runs through the account of Elijah and the widow's only son (1 Kg 17:17-24), and Elisha with another mother's son (2 Kg 4:17-20, 32-37), and with Naaman (2 Kg 5:8-15), and Hezekiah's never-to-be-forgotten story (2 Kg 20:1-11; Is 38:1-21).

It runs through Asa's failure to ask for needed healing, and Nebuchadnezzar's recovery from insanity by direct touch (Dn 4:24-37), and Jonah's grateful experience with that shady palm, and his remarkable preservation inside the huge fish.

David's heart repeatedly rings out the same

theme (Ps 6:2; 30:2-3; 34:20; 41:2-3; 91:3-7, 10-13). One passage in particular reveals the fullness and richness of the healing theme (Ps 103:1-5). Let me paraphrase it to make the meaning in David's mind a bit clearer.

Who forgives all your iniquities;

Who heals all your diseases;

Who keeps you from going down to the grave before your full span of life is run out;

Who crowns you with loving kindness and tender mercies;

Who satisfies your matured years [when mental and spiritual depression is apt to come] with the renewal of vigor until you are as eager in spirit as an eagle soaring through the vast aerial heights.

David names five kinds of healing. The first is spiritual. The fourth refers to the outer circumstances of one's life. The other three refer specifically to bodily health and vigor.

There's a choice verse from the pen of Solomon, the wisest of men. The revision gives this, "a tranquil heart is the life of the flesh" (Prv 14:30). Literally it reads, "the life of the body? a quiet heart."

The processes of grace are fascinating. Full

touch with God gives the quiet heart what passes mere mental understanding and what in turn acts directly on all the bodily functions. The trail runs eagerly ahead into the future glories never out of the Hebrew vision. The coming Messiah-King is to bring physical blessings, along with all others.

Isaiah's exultant song of the coming day (Is 35) may be taken as an index to the long list. The blind and the deaf, the lame and the dumb, will see all these disabilities leave (Is 35:5-6).

Ezekiel's remarkable river, from trickling beginnings to flood, carried exuberant physical life and healing everywhere. And the leaves of the trees it fed would be a healing potion for all (Ez 47:9, 12).

The whole of the Old Testament makes one rhythmic answer to our question. They reveal plainly and graphically *God's attitude*. He not only can heal, but it is his eager wish to do so. His love outruns his power.

Always there is the eager reaching through bodily healing to the deeper, the richer, the spirit healing. The disciplinary side of suffering is plain. It's a wooing process. Through these silent pleadings and teachings of suffering, God reaches in for the deeper.

Teaching for Church Days

The Bible most intimately reveals the one unchanging nature of God. He is ever the same.

The Book of Acts best illustrates this nature with the epistles woven in, and the Revelation knot on the end.

In the Gospels, Christ reveals the heart of the Father. He vividly gives the meaning of the Old Testament pages. Acts continues the story, for all the peoples of all the world who come into living touch with the heart of Christ.

Acts is the sequel to the Gospels. The Gospels are sample pages of the coming kingdom time, while sample pages of the church time are found in Acts. Each covers a generation of time.

In the Gospels the King is pleading for acceptance. His ministry is an eloquent plea. In all he does, he is saying, "this is a bit of what the kingdom is like." But the King is rejected and goes voluntarily to the cross to give his life for men and for their sins. Then something new comes in. It is never spoken of in the Old Testament. It fills in the interregnum until the King shall bring in the kingdom. The messenger-nation fails.

A new group is formed to be God's new messenger to the race. It is called the church, the "taken-out" group. It is made up of all believers in Christ, both Jew and non-Jew, by the Holy Spirit's presence.

There's a natural contrast or comparison between the Gospels and the Acts. The Gospels are kingdom pages; the Acts the church book. Acts runs through a generation of time, roughly thirty-three years. Then it breaks abruptly off, as though each generation of the church should carry on the story, until Christ comes for the next step in his program.

In the Gospels, healing has the foremost place in Christ's activity. But it does not become prominent until Christ's rejection by the leaders is made clear. There's over a year of waiting for national acceptance. Then John the Baptist, Christ's official herald, is imprisoned, foreshadowing Christ's own rejection.

Christ first turns to Galilee, unofficial Galilee, despised by the cultured Jerusalem leaders. He begins preaching and teaching and healing the crowds and training the inner group of disciples.

When the national rejection of his messiahship is clear, he turns to the personal side of the Messiah's work. Healing now takes the prominent place. It is through healing that he first attracts the great thronging crowds.

In Acts healing has a distinct place, but on the whole not as prominent a place as in the Gospels. It becomes only one feature of the gracious ministry described and of the power experienced. Is *is* one feature. It is distinct in itself. Yet it becomes one feature with the others.

Acts contains five summaries of healings. These indicate that vast crowds experienced healing. All sorts of cases were included, and a great power was clearly in action, having a deep abiding spiritual effect on the people.

There are eight individual instances of healing. One could be classed as acute. One involved the supernatural protection from a deadly viper. Six are incorrigible incurables: twice lameness from birth, one of forty years standing; once long-standing palsy; twice the dead are brought back to life; and possibly Paul's recovery from stoning would be included with this last item.

There are two outstanding centers of healing activity: Jerusalem, the Jewish center, and Ephesus, the Gentile or non-Jewish center. The Jerusalem activity is at the beginning and the Ephesus activity distinctly toward the close of the Acts period.

At Jerusalem great crowds are healed, great healing power is in evidence, and great spiritual blessing is connected with the healing. At Ephesus the activity runs through two full years. The power in evidence is unusual, and the spiritual power in men's lives is pronounced.

Ephesus was the strategic center of Asia Minor. The message preached, and the power revealed there, went out to all parts of Asia Minor and across the seas in every direction.

It is interesting to note that healing has greater prominence in the record, in the space given it, at the beginning of Acts. It is comparable to the healing ministry in the Gospels. It remains a distinct part of the activity until the abrupt ending of Acts.

One is conscious that healing becomes one feature of the Book of Acts. The absorbing thing here is the preaching of the crucified and risen Christ. The healing becomes one manifestation with others of the power of the risen Christ.

Yet, there is no suggestion of the lessening of the power in healing, nor of minimizing its place. For it is toward the close of the Acts period that the unusual story is told of the young man who fell out of the window at Troas and died, and was restored to life. And the outstanding Ephesus campaign is likewise toward the close. It is merely a shift of proportionate emphasis.

The Epistles fit into the pages of Acts and are most intelligently read and understood when they are read in that way. They run side by side with Acts, with Revelation coming a bit later as the knot at the end of the whole.

Corinth becomes the strategic center of European activity, as Ephesus is the strategic center of the Asiatic. As Ephesus had a special message of healing *activity,* Corinth sends out a special message of healing *teaching*. Much space is given to the active ministry of the whole group of disciples in Corinth. It was clearly an active church center, with the power of the Holy Spirit at work.

Much attention is given to teaching about

healing. Healing was blessedly common in the experience of the Corinthian Christians. And many among them had the power to minister to those in bodily suffering.

Healing is spoken of as one of the nine or more special gifts of the Holy Spirit. It was given to some, but not to all. Here is the same sense of proportionate emphasis as in the Book of Acts. It was a blessed gift, one of several. Paul puts special emphasis on balanced teaching and keeping things in proportion.

Toward the close of this Acts-Paul period, there is mentioning of some not healed. Paul's thorn comes in here. These are treated in the story of "God's School of Suffering" (see chapter 7), as part of the disciplinary side of suffering. The thing to notice just now is that they in no way change or affect the main teaching about healing. They simply give light to keep things in balance.

For centuries, a common teaching has been that miracles ceased long ago and are not to be expected today. And this includes healing. The Book of Acts, with the interwoven Epistles, gives the clear answer. The interwoven Acts and Epistles make up the church book, indicating that healing is meant to be a common occurrence to the end of the church period.

From the outer non-Jewish world, where these letters mostly take us, there is a quick turn back to things at the Jewish center.

The first Bishop of Jerusalem reveals the custom and the teaching that continued in the old mother church. Teaching on healing did not lessen nor did the blessed experience of it (Jas 5:13-15).

Then the circle of this wondrous old twin-book of God swings back to the starting point. A garden grows at both ends, Genesis and Revelation. God's ideal persists clear to the end and becomes real, actual. The tree of life has become a grove of trees. The garden has become a garden-city. All the fine simplicity of the country and the garden is coupled with all the fine, true culture for which the city characteristically stands.

The same is true regarding our bodies. Sickness and pain, tears and death, mourning and crying, these are gone. The trees of life bear monthly harvests, and their leaves, like Ezekiel's, are for healing (Rv 21:4, 22:1-2).

The Answer of the Book

All this simply gives us a picture of God, a portrait in oil, in warm living colors. That is the one point of the question we are asking. What sort of a God is he? What is he willing to do? It is not a question of power, but of his willingness, his purpose. Not *can* he? But *will* he?

The picture in the Old Testament is enough to answer the question. The warmer colors of a living Man underscore the answer in bright red. The tenderness, the sympathetic heart, the eagerness of God, take hold of one's heart as his Only-Begotten actually becomes one of us.

So we come back to that sentence stated at the first. *It is God's first will that we should be pure in heart, gripped by a nobly strong purpose, balanced in our understanding of things, humanly gentle in our personal contacts, at sweet peace within, content in circumstances, and hearty and healthy in our bodies.*

But note that word "first," God's *first* will. There will be a "quiet talk" devoted entirely to the meaning of the word "first." That's a doorway into God's schoolroom (see chapter 7).

Christ does heal today. It is his eager will to do so, and to do it now. One may reach out his hand and receive what healing he needs, now as he is reading, *so far as God's is concerned.* If there be any delay, it need not be longer than it takes for a man to come into full touch with God.

In healing, Christ is thinking of two things, always two. The first impresses us most, if we are needing it. The second is really the thing of greater meaning. Christ wants to heal our bodies. He wants to heal our spirits, our lives, our real selves. He wants to do the first, but in such a way as to include the greater thing, the second.

The first is delayed sometimes, often, until we are willing for the second to happen. But the length of the delay is fixed by us. Christ eagerly reaches out to do both for each of us now.

There is one exception to be noted. We are never promised immunity from bodily death. There are three instances in the Gospels of the dead restored, and two, possibly a third, in the Acts. Yet, the plain teaching throughout does not include this. A part of the promise definitely made is that through the touch of Christ on the body, the full span of natural life will be filled out. (Note Ps 103:4f; Ex 23:26; Dt 4:40, 32:47.)

So far as death itself is concerned, the resurrection of our bodies at some future day is plainly taught for those believers who do not live until Christ's return. The teaching does not go beyond these two items.

Now from the other book, the book of illustrations, the Book of Life.

A friend of mine told me about his experience of bodily healing. It's a double story. He is a business man, well known in the city where he lives and active in Christian service.

While in his thirties, he suffered a stroke and paralysis, as a result of overwork. It affected one side. His arm hung limp, though not wholly disabled. He could walk some, dragging his limb. Because he lost muscle control in his face, spittle would ooze out of his mouth. The writing on the pages of his diary at this time was scarcely legible.

He went to a friend, a physician, who taught that Christ heals by direct touch. The friend made a very simple brief prayer for his healing. My friend limped out of the other's home, as he had limped in, and started back to his own home. As he was painfully dragging his foot along, he felt a sense of warmth come into his body, running through his affected side, down the arm, and out his fingertips. He knew the healing touch had come.

He entered his home with his latchkey, and his wife came running to meet him, and then stopped short. She looked startled and said, "Oh, Frank, you have been healed!"

My friend had an unusually intimate relationship with his pastor who lived near him. The pastor had suffered for years from heart trouble. He had applied repeatedly for life insurance with various companies, but had always been rejected because of his heart. Now, my friend went to see his pastor and told his story of what had just occurred to him. They spent some time praising God and praying together.

The pastor was deeply impressed because of his own need. After meeting with my friend, he spent much time alone in his study on his knees with the open Bible. He felt within that he should believe the healing touch had come. Again he applied for life insurance, was examined with the usual rigid care, and now was accepted.

He began to speak of healing in his preaching. But it was not acceptable to his denominational leaders. So it was not taught in any outstanding way and gradually slipped out of his preaching.

He afterward became president of a leading Methodist university, was later made bishop, and became prominent in the broader counsels and activity of his communion. I had the privilege of his personal acquaintance in later years.

My friend, a soft-spoken methodical businessman, told me the story quietly, with a businessman's care in details. He has led a very busy life since, and seems to be in perfect health. His story seems like an added page to the unfinished Book of Acts. Clearly there would be many more such pages added if our great Christ had his way with us.

THREE

Does God Send Sickness and Disease?

It is God's first will that every man be clean in heart, in the grip of a noble purpose, clear in understanding of things, at peace within himself, gentle in spirit, happy in circumstances, and strong and vigorous in his body.

Essentials and Incidentals

Christ was and is a man of power. This is his distinctive characteristic. His is power under the driving control of love.

The religion of Christ is a religion of power. This is its outstanding feature. It was through this that Christianity won its way in the beginning, in the bitter competition with old entrenched religions. It was this power that blazed its way into every nation and civilization where it has gone.

It is a power clearly above any power human

beings are accustomed to. It is distinctly greater than men have known. It rises above power that works through national channels.

So it is called supernatural power. It was plainly claimed to be the power of Christ himself, and of God in Christ at work through natural channels. And always it came into play to help men. The help was sorely needed. Men were powerless to do what was needed.

This more-than-natural power of Christ and of Christianity met men's need with a strange, glad fullness. It was this distinctive trait that opened doors and hearts and lives where the power was felt and seen.

Christianity is not a code of ethics, simply. It is that, plainly. It leaves all other codes trailing behind. Indeed there is clear evidence that all these other codes sprang out of the mother roots of Christianity. But, by comparison, this is merely a by-product, a blessed by-product. Supernatural power is what makes Christianity distinctive.

It is not merely a system of culture, though it is cultural. The Holy Spirit's sway in a life brings the rarest culture of character and conduct. It leads to the truest culture of mind and personality and life. And this multiplied in many individual lives makes a rarely cultured community.

Christian culture is the culture of heart and motive and behavior and outreach to others. It out-cultures all other cultures familiar to man. Its culture, at root, planted and fertilized all real culture wherever and whenever found.

But, in comparison with the central character-istic of true Christianity, its culture is incidental, a winsome, wondrous incidental. The essential trait goes deeper in and reaches farther out. Its power to transform personal life stands first and alone.

Christianity is not only a teaching and a philosophy. But it includes teaching, and it is a pervasive and satisfying philosophy. All men and all philosophers and all nations that know it, gladly speak of it and imitate it.

There is evidence for believing that all other philosophies and teachings run back to the Hebraic roots from which Christianity grew. And this is still true, regardless of the strange unhallowed admixtures in these other systems.

Yet, again this is not the chief aspect of Christianity. There is something greater than this. It is so much greater that it has no second. It is in a class by itself. Christianity is a thing of more-than-natural, more-than-human, power. It reveals God's own power in action through natural human channels.

Christianity is not a humanitarianism, a scheme for bettering world conditions, simply. But it works to better the world.

A simple look back into history to pre-

Christian times and a quick look at non-Christian civilizations today reveal a startling contrast between nations that have come under Christian influence and the others who haven't.

Humanitarianism in all its forms, and the unselfish bettering of outer conditions, stand out so big under the Christian touch that it seems almost absent elsewhere. Yet the distinct though faint traces elsewhere, even though untraceable directly, bear every mark of springing from the same Eden-Hebrew-Christian roots. Christ's humanitarianism is the root, actually, of all humanitarian ideals.

Still, a moment's clear, sharp thinking makes quite plain that humanitarian ideals that have meant so much and still do beyond all calculation, are incidentals.

They are the sweet, refreshing fragrance of the rose. The rose itself, creating fragrance and lavishingly breathing it out into the sweetened air, is quite another thing. The rose is always immeasurably greater than the fragrance it gives unselfishly out to all corners.

Power: the Distinctive Trait

Christianity itself, in its one outstanding characteristic, is immeasurably more than the humanitarianism it initiates and sustains. Its singular outstanding trait is its supernatural power, found nowhere else. It does what no other religion does or can do.

Without supernatural power, in our understanding and our teaching of Christianity, the essence is gone. The fragrance is here; the rose is gone. How long will the fragrance linger with its source cut off?

If and when our Christianity becomes a code of ethics merely, a culture and only that, a teaching and philosophy and nothing more, a blessed humanitarianism and a bettering of the outward conditions of life, and that simply, the distinctive trait will have gone. The rose is severed from the fragrance. The life has gone out of the body, even with some color in the cheek, and some muscular movements in the limbs still present.

All these other things, so blessed in themselves, are mere by-products of Christianity, incidentals. One might call them trifling incidentals, by comparison, though they are valuable in themselves.

Christianity is distinctively, intrinsically, a thing of power, supernatural power, God's own direct touch through natural human channels. The lustful man is made pure. The slave of evil habit is set free. The thief becomes honest. The trifler becomes earnest in the hard grip of a noble purpose. The drunkard is sobered and stays sober. The demon-tortured man knows sweet peace. The diseased is made perfectly whole.

Where there had been a man in the house, now there is a loving husband and a thoughtful father in a home. And the shop or store, the neighborhood, the community, the nation, each knows a radical difference, a new personality, which is strong, gentle, pervasive, insistent.

The religion of the solitary God-Man who died, and then revealed unprecedented and unparalleled power, in emptying that new-hewn tomb of rock, is a religion of supernatural power. It is a power inexplicable except by taking God into account.

It makes changes in man. It changes things at the core. Then all becomes changed. All history and all observation and all experience show that significant changes can't be made by any other person than Christ himself. Christianity is distinctively a religion of supernatural power.

The one purpose of foreign missionary activity is to carry this message of the Christ to our fellow human beings who haven't heard. It is the message of a Christ who died as none other did, nor could, nor can, and then lived again through supernatural power, and still lives with that same supernatural power available today to purify the heart, transform the life, and meet every common need.

This was the one burning passion and purpose of early missionary activity, and it still is, where the Holy Spirit holds sway. It burns so hotly and grips so strongly that all else seems incidental. There are humanitarian activities immeasurably valuable and sorely needed. Western science has aided in easing the suffering of the third world. And that sort of thing is surely needed. Yet there needs to be discretion.

It is not part of the Christian missionary scheme to transplant Western civilization into Oriental lands. The Orient has a culture of its own, and some of us Occidentals think it is at least fully equal to Western culture and in some things superior. If our missionary activity becomes a mere transplanting of certain features of the Western hemisphere to Eastern and sub-equatorial lands, it at once loses its historical Christian characteristic. The essence will be gone.

If the door opened with such sacrifice by the early heroic missionaries becomes an entrance for some common features of our Western civilization, if it becomes a means of spreading Western skepticism and doubt under Christian phraseology, it is surely the Devil using that door. Such use would make the door a curse. The motive for such sacrifice as the true Christian missionary gladly makes, though it slowly takes his life's blood, will be gone.

The true Christian message lived and taught on foreign-mission soil, in the supernatural power of the Holy Spirit, brings certain results. Out of it will grow naturally the true Christian culture. *And* out of that will grow the mental and spiritual regeneration that will affect daily life and conditions.

Nowhere is the distinctively supernatural power of Christ revealed more than in this, that men's bodies are healed. It was so in Christ's day on earth. It was so in the early church days. It is so today. Christ is still and ever the same.

Of course, there is opposition to such a Christ, and to Christianity. It was vigorous in Christ's day. It was bitter, incorrigible, malicious, and at last murderous.

A False Common Impression

That opposition hasn't ceased. It has merely changed its outer form. It has grown more cultured on the outside, but the inside is the same. One phase of this opposition is the teaching that God sends sickness and disease. The bald statement gives an ugly impression of God that stings and stays. It hurts and it lasts. A deep dread of a God and of his irresistible power arises inside. This is so even among saintly Christians, far more than is suspected.

Its practical effect has been to act as a check, to prevent Christ's supernatural power from working in our lives. The hand doesn't reach out to take what the pierced hand is eagerly reaching down to give. There is a deep-seated impression that we cannot ask for healing. We must settle down and make the best of a bad thing. Meanwhile, we pray to be patient and resigned.

Psychologically this becomes an unconscious, incalculable influence in actually tightening the hold of disease on one's body. Practically it is a hindrance to God's rare supernatural power working in our bodies, and in our lives.

"Well, it was her time to go, and so God sent her pneumonia." The words were spoken quietly, in a matter-of-fact way and in a tone of finality. They were the answer to my sympathetic question about an earnest Christian woman in the prime of life who had died quite unexpectedly.

I wondered if my startled ears heard right. But my wife verified their accuracy. The woman who spoke the words was an earnest Christian.

In later conversation a neighbor of hers, who did not share her belief in this regard, remarked that this was a common thought among the Christians of the area. In varying degree, one finds such deep-seated impression everywhere.

Certainly there are statements in the scriptures that can be distorted and disconnected to give such an impression. Most often there is no intention of distorting the scriptures, but they are read in a haphazard, disjointed way, and quoted without regard to context.

The Teaching of the Bible

Let us take a brief look at the Bible on this point. There's a long list of passages that, taken by themselves, at first glance do give that impression. But as we read them in connection with the whole teaching, we will feel ashamed to have misunderstood God's word and maligned God's character.

When Abraham and Sarah went into Egypt, "Jehovah plagued Pharaoh and his household with great plagues because of Sarah, Abraham's wife" (Gn 12:10-20). The word "plagues" here plainly means certain contagious diseases common in Egypt.

The story explains why the plagues were sent. God's plan for the new nation hinged on Abraham, and even more on his wife and on the family stock being kept pure. There was an emergency in the working out of the human plan. The broader view of the story reverses the impression of God randomly inflicting disease upon the Egyptians. Still the impression is there, to the unthinking.

God's dealings with Pharaoh in delivering Israel from Egyptian slavery is another commonly misunderstood story. I haven't the space or time to delve into this whole story of judgment on the Egyptians for their conduct toward God and toward the Hebrews. But it plainly says that it was through "the hand of the Lord" in direct action that the Egyptian cattle were fatally diseased, and the Hebrews' cattle immune; the ulcerous boils upon the Egyptians themselves, and so on, through all the plagues that follow (Ex 9:1-7, 8-12).

One notes, of course, that this is all a distinctly exceptional act of judgment in a crisis. It is not the normal response of God. Still the impression of a pain-inflicting God may remain if one doesn't think the story out as plainly taught. And so there is a string of similar passages (Ex 15:25-26; 32:35; Lv 10:1-2; Nm 11:1, 33; 12:9-15; 14:12, 36-37; Dt 28:21-22, 27, 35, 60, 61).

The story of Jacob's hip being put out of joint is an exception (Gn 32:24-32). One notes at once that it was not a disease, but a touch that affected the normal action of his body, his walking. It slowed him up, and became a constant reminder that he *had been* walking the wrong way. Afterwards, though his walking was slower, it was in God's way, the only right way.

It stands out as an exception, because it was not until after all other means had failed that God put Jacob's hip out of joint. Jacob was an unusually stubborn man. It was for service's sake, and it was done because Jacob, who was the center of God's world plan, was hindering the unfolding of that plan. It will be spoken of again in the chapter on "God's School of Suffering."

The Protected Zone

There are two things to note here in order to keep the balance, and to get things straight and clear. The first and lesser thing is that any break with God takes one away from the protection of his presence, and so automatically exposes him to whatever conditions surround him.

It's natural to *keep in touch* with God. His mere presence, in unbroken touch, is a continual protection from ills that surround us. It is his touch that keeps our bodies strong and functioning naturally and vigorously.

This teaching is like an ever-present undertone through the older pages of the Bible. It was true in Eden and through all Bible history. It is true today. This is the continual background of all the Old Testament teaching about bodily conditions.

One simple illustration may help, but it is only one from a long list of others. It is given because it is a picture, an open window into the whole Book.

It is the graphically told story of the unnamed prophet in the First Book of Kings (1 Kgs 13). He had been sent to King Jeroboam at a critical time, with a message and with detailed instructions concerning his own conduct. Clearly his conduct in the particulars named was to be an acted-out part of the message.

Another prophet, merely a professional

prophet, jealously deceived the man with God's message, and, as a result, the unnamed prophet disobeyed God's explicit instructions. Because of this deception the unnamed prophet returned home by the way he was distinctly forbidden by God to take and was slain by a lion.

The whole story is dramatically told in much detail and the whole nation knew the story and discussed it from door to door.

The teaching that we should note particularly is that this unnamed prophet, by disobeying God's implicit directions, *had gone out of the protected zone.*

When in touch with God, the prophet was in the protected zone. No evil could befall him in the simple path of obedience. He was protected. When he left that path, he was exposed to the dangers always in the world.

The natural human life is meant to be lived with heart and life in touch with God. Anything else is abnormal, unnatural. When in touch with God, one is constantly protected and preserved and strengthened, in body and circumstance and life.

Break with God, either partial or full, exposes one to whatever there is of evil, and to the Evil One. Unfortunately, many Christians do not live in full, simple, intelligent touch with Christ in all their affairs.

This is the background of all teaching in the Old Testament. Unhappily it is a teaching often missed in the haphazard, unconnected, choppy reading of the Bible, so common in pew and pulpit, home and study.

The Bible, taken as a whole, is always self-explanatory. Any question it raises concerning its meaning is always answered somewhere else in the Book. Every thoughtful, serious question has an answer there somewhere. If only we would *read* it, and read it *intelligently as a whole,* as one connected book, it would flood us with its light at every turn.

But the second thing stands out plainly before all eyes. It is the bigger thing of the two. It is the Book of Job. The story of Job deals directly with this question of sickness and disease, the source and the purpose.

The Book of Job tells plainly that the troubles that came to Job, including his ulcerous boils at the last, came directly from Satan (Jb 1:12-19, 2:6-7). Job himself, though, did not understand the source, and ascribed them to God (Jb 1:20-21, 2:10).

They came by God's permission. There were sharply defined limits to Satan's activity, beyond which he could not, dared not, go (Jb 1:12; 2:6). God had a purpose for giving the permission. It was distinctly a purpose of love. Then the healing came (see Jb 33:15-25; 42:10-17). The gracious flood of blessing that followed made the days of his earlier prosperity seem tame.

That in a word is the Job story. It is further discussed in the chapter on "God's School of Suffering." But the teaching could not be clearer. It answers our present question. It answers it fully and plainly. And the teaching stands out clearly in God's Book, so that all who will simply read thoughtfully may understand.

The Source of Disease

God does not send disease and sickness. The answer given in the Bible to the question of suffering includes five parts:

1. They come through some open door of disobedience to the laws of the body, either a conscious or an unconscious disobedience.

2. They may come directly from Satan, but always *through* some open door on the human side.

3. They may come through God's restraint being withdrawn.

4. They may come through the general break of sin affecting the whole fabric of life.

5. There may be a blend of two or more of these.

In each case, there must be an open door on the human side. But, then, open doors are certainly there on every hand in great abundance.

God does not need to send disease to discipline people. Most of us, through disobedience, leave doors standing invitingly open to disease. Disobedience of the common laws of health is the most common, even among the most earnest Christians. More will be said about this in the chapter on "The Human Side of Health and Healing."

We don't seem to realize that breaking a law of one's body, though not against a moral law, takes on a distinctly moral quality. The laws of health are God's laws for the body, as truly as moral laws are his for our inner life.

God's healing, it will be remembered, is threefold. One aspect of it is a protective restraint on disease and other physical afflictions. Another is a life-giving, health-giving touch upon one's body. The very absence of bodily ills and weakness should be cause for praise. It reveals Christ's direct touch, when the body is committed to his care.

The third aspect arises when sickness or disease actually comes, perhaps through some door left inadvertently open, or otherwise. It is the supernatural healing touch.

When one is led to meet some emergency that taxes or exposes one's health unduly, special strength will be given. But one should be certain of God's leading here. Once it is clear that God is leading us, we can push confidently on, depending on Christ for bodily strength, as for everything else.

Bodily doors should be as carefully guarded as all others. Spiritual warfare is being waged. And one needs to be constantly on guard. In a wholesome, sane, thoughtful way, we should each guard all the doorways of our lives. This is especially true of those wholly in Christian service.

John Ruskin tells a simple incident from his childhood days, which illustrates in part what we are talking about. He was present one afternoon when tea was being served. The bright copper hot-water kettle caught the child's eye. He wanted to touch it, and reached out his hand. The nurse in attendance on the child told him not to. The boy persisted, and the nurse also persisted.

By and by the mother said quietly, "Nurse, let him touch it." He did, for a very brief moment. His curiosity was quickly satisfied. His attention was turned from the kettle to his finger.

The child's ignorant persistence in having his own way, regardless of the expressed wish of those in authority, was deliberately yielded to—for a purpose. The restraint was withdrawn. The act of touching the kettle contained its own punishment in the pain that came. The child had learned something. His desire to touch shining copper kettles was satisfied forever.

But some of us haven't as much sense. We still want to touch the shiny kettle. God's commands and laws are never arbitrary. He doesn't simply want to be obeyed because he has the right to be. Though when you come to know him, you recognize that this would be sufficient in itself.

But God's commands always take into consideration our well-being. God would keep us from touching the hot kettle, because it will burn. This principle underlies every law and commandment God gives.

An English friend recounted an experience she had while engaged in missionary work in Algiers. An emergency made it necessary for her to nurse a typhus patient for a brief time under quarantine regulations.

When the patient was taken to the hospital, my friend bathed, changed her garments, and took every precaution known to her. Then she retired for much-needed sleep. She had a dream, unusually vivid and distinct in detail. She was out riding, and saw a conflict going on between one of her missionary associates and three persons. She seemed to know instinctively that one of these three was the Devil.

She hastened forward to help her associate, but a dart was thrown by one of the three, and her associate fell as she came between them. Almost mechanically she prayed, repeating the words "the power of the blood of Jesus."

At once the three fell back. Then they came again to the attack. Again she prayed, repeating that same phrase, but apparently without realizing its full significance and power. And again the three fell back.

A third time they pressed the attack. Then it came to her swiftly, with an intense sense of reality, just what power there was in that prayer, pleading "the power of the blood of Jesus."

Pleading it now boldly, strongly, insistently, she saw the three crouched down and back as though struck. Then slowly, reluctantly, but surely, they disappeared. And her associate was free of their power.

That was the unusual dream. She awoke with a high fever. Then the significance of the dream seemed borne in upon her.

She began to pray tensely and insistently, pleading the power of the blood of Jesus. Then sleep came, quiet and deep. When she awoke the second time, the fever was gone. Her pulse and temperature were normal. She was cool and well. And with a grateful heart she went about her day's task.

Let us keep in touch with the heart and life of Christ, guard jealously all the doors, set ourselves to keep in that protected zone of obedience, *and,* when the need comes, go at once to Christ.

Christ is waiting now, at your side, with the touch of supernatural power, to meet every need of body and life.

FOUR

How Does Christ Heal?

It is Christ's first will for his followers, that they be pure in heart, steadily passionate in purpose, balanced in understanding and judgment, characteristically gentle in personal touches, willing to be controlled in everything by the emergency of sin in the world, and healthful and vigorous in body, to his glory.

Natural and Supernatural

God is cautious about using the supernatural. He is lavish in nature. Nature is God in action. He loves nature's roads. He made them, and he prefers them. But he will not hesitate for a moment to do the supernatural when the need calls for it. He will do a fresh act of creation, pure direct creation, before a single line of his word is allowed to fail.

He will reach through and above the natural

channels with the added touch before he will let one trusting child of his, in intelligent touch of heart and will, know disappointment. Supernatural power responds more quickly than natural power to emergencies that plainly call for it.

Nevertheless, God loves nature's regular paths. They are his own. Nature is God's way of working things out. Christ avoids the sensational, the cheap, the vulgar. On more than one occasion he wanted to avoid the crowd that cried out for some touch of this morbid sort of sensationalism.

Even so, nothing is so sensational, in the good sense, as God's supernatural power in action in an emergency. Christ's miraculous healing created a tremendous sensation. And he made use of that sensation to teach of the Father's eager love and gentle patience and lavish power.

The supernatural has a touch of the spectacular, because we are not used to it. It is unusual. It catches attention at once. The natural hardly gets any attention, because we are used to it.

Nature is simple and quiet. The things that mean most to us, and to our daily lives, come noiselessly, softly. They work modestly. No one ever heard the sun or the moon, busily at work keeping the whole order of nature in blessed rhythm for our sakes. The dew does its gracious work shyly. It is the small, warm, gentle rain that the soil welcomes most and responds to most quickly. The air carries out its unfailing ministry so modestly, we scarcely ever think of its presence, till some foul intruder spoils its sweet odor and neutralizes its life-giving power.

Truth is always simple. It wears a plain garb and talks in gentle speech. It never calls attention to itself. It passes almost unnoticed in the bustle of the street. But it breathes out a healthful atmosphere and leaves a fragrant trail.

Error wears flashy clothes. It talks in loud, boisterous tones. It blusters and swaggers the full width of the sidewalk. And the crowd stops and stares and doesn't realize that the air has been tainted. Error masquerades in a costume of truth or else it would easily be discovered.

The Devil borrows truth's clothes, without asking permission. He talks in a loud, positive, there's-no-doubt-about-it voice. So men's eyes and ears may be caught and befouled.

The sheeplike quality persists in us. Watch a flock of sheep. They'll follow the bellwether unhesitatingly, even over the side of the bridge into the rushing river. Cheap, noisy leadership quickly draws the crowd.

Nature is simple. That's God's touch. Satan tangles things up. Truth is so simple that it seems too easy sometimes. One instinctively says "of course." Sin makes life's problems complex. Truth is plain-spoken and unpretentious.

Christ is cautious about the supernatural. He is

lavish in nature. He gives so lavishly that there would be no need of the supernatural, if it were not for the urgent crises of life.

Sin is forever setting life askew, and creating emergencies. A single touch of the supernatural quickly catches the eye. The abundance of the natural at work all around us rarely gets a thought.

Yet, though already so lavish in his giving, Christ is eager to give the more-than-common touch of power, the supernatural, when need be.

Sin's ravages are epidemic. There's a willful ignorance of the simple, natural laws of the body. There's an ignorant disregard of nature's benefi-cent laws of action. There's a constant need of the supernatural touch. And Christ thoughtfully gives that touch in the way that will help us best and most.

Our well-being, body and spirit, is precious to him. He holds sacred the integrity of his pledged word. He is on the heels of evil, like a flash, before any trusting child of his shall be disappointed, or an iota of his word allowed to go unfulfilled.

Helping in Order Not to Hurt

We have been talking about Christ's power in healing; what he *can* do. We have spoken of his love in healing; what he *will* do, and do with an eager gladness. Now, we want to talk a bit together about Christ's wisdom in healing, the *way* in which he does heal. There's a rare wisdom in Christ's method in healing men's bodies.

To give in order to help, and help in the best way, and help only, not hurt, is a fine art indeed. Nothing is more ticklishly difficult. Thoughtless giving is cheap and common, lazy and hurtful. Love is always thoughtful, though it costs more. But love ignores the cost even when it must be counted.

In his healing, Christ is thinking always of two things, the immediate need and the deeper need, the body, and the man himself living in the body. Often, helping the deeper need meets the bodily need too, and meets it in the best way. The glad, intelligent surrender to Christ as Master brings certain changes in one's habits. And this in turn often radically affects the body and the health.

Christ's touch upon the life prepares the way for the touch upon the body. Yet it does more. It leads to intelligent thinking. And this in turn leads to such obedience to the laws of the body that a recurrence of bodily trouble is prevented.

Sometimes obedience is simple. Sometimes it is radical. It may mean breaking old habits in such common things as eating and sleeping and the methodical daily round. Health and healing are dependent on these commonalities.

Christ is love. And nowhere is love more strenuously tested than in giving. The tangle of sin blurs our eyes, and teeters our judgment this way or that, and especially twists our will.

Two things should be especially noted about how Christ heals: the how of *conditions* and the how of *method*.

The conditions underlie all else. This has to do with one's touch with Christ. The method has to do with the healing itself, the way the healing is done. The physician and the sick person must get in touch. Christ and the person needing Christ's healing power must get together.

Some people suppose that saintliness is the requirement for the healing touch. They suppose that only the saintly may come and expect the healing touch.

Of course, the closer the touch the better. And saintliness implies a close touch. But it isn't the saintliness that heals. It is Christ, Christ's blood, that heals.

It is never because of any merit in us that we are healed. It is *through* the contact, however saintly it may or may not be, that Christ's healing power comes in.

The "How" of Conditions

Now, the word *about the conditions* necessary for healing. Of course, there are always conditions. That's part of life. Whether driving through thick traffic in the city, cooking a good meal, playing golf, or keeping in good physical shape, conditions are always involved.

Here the conditions are so simple that they are almost laughable. Yet they are so inflexibly rigid that they are absolutely indispensable, like most conditions of life.

Listen to the conditions: come to Christ the Savior, who died for your sins, as none other did, nor could, nor can. Ask for, and accept, forgiveness of your sins and the cleansing from sin through his blood. Thank him for dying for you and taking your sin away.

Then, when the need comes, go at once to him. Whatever the need may be: cleansing from some sin you have let in, power to break that evil habit, guidance in some difficult situation, or bodily healing of whatever sort, to whatever extent, go to him. Go first to him. Go to him at once.

He will forgive all your iniquities. He will heal all your diseases. He will prolong your days till the full span of life is run out. He will put his direct helpful touch on the outer circumstances, for your sake. He will renew the vigor of body and mind and spirit up to the measure it should be. This is his will for you and me (Ps 103:1-5).

It would be enough to stop right here. This covers all the conditions to be met. But, because things are a bit foggy, it will be good to talk about just what this means in actual habit, in the common run of daily life.

We haven't been taught about healing. Indeed we haven't been taught much at all about the Christian life, though there are always fine exceptions. We need to be taught in order to gain an intelligent understanding. The fruits of teaching are matured mental judgment and a seasoned wisdom to know how to act in emergencies.

We will know how to meet opposition. We will understand about "the fiery darts." For our enemy is cunning and practiced. He is an old hand in the fine art of fooling, and filling the air with foggy questions and doubts.

An old seasoned soldier holds steady under fire when the new recruit takes to his heels. The experienced banker or broker keeps his head when panic threatens where the less-seasoned takes fright and maybe loses out.

This wisdom is summed up in four words, an *act,* a *purpose,* a *habit,* an *attitude.* The *act* is the surrender to Christ as a Master, not a Savior simply, but a Master. In a thoughtful, intelligent, seasoned way, Christ is to be allowed to sway all the habits, as the flame sways the dry kindling in the grate with a good draft.

The personal habits, the home relationships and contacts, the daily work, or business or profession, the recreations and social contacts— all these, in a wholesome, sane, habitual way, are to be as you believe Christ would prefer. For he always has a decided preference. When in doubt, hold the thing in question open till the doubt clears. Then, surrender.

The surrender begins as an act, a glad act. Then it becomes a practice, a constant unwavering practice. Then it becomes a habit, a fixed unconscious habit of action. It simply means fullest touch of habit and motive and life with him who died for us, out of the love of his heart, when he didn't have to. This is the meaning of being *in touch with Christ*.

The *purpose* to please him in everything. The purpose really becomes a passion, a tender, strong, intense passion, a passion of love, a passion for *him*.

It does not simply ask "is this wrong?" or "is this right?" But it asks, "What would he prefer? What would please him?" A thing may be proven not to be wrong. But if that quiet inner voice tells you it is not best, not what he would prefer, then that is conclusive for the man really *in touch*.

The *habit* is spending a bit of time alone with the Bible every day. The day may be crowded, but the one *in touch* finds that bit of time growing longer of itself rather than shorter. What one really desires can always be fit into the schedule, however crowded the day and the way.

This daily time will be time when the mind is fresh, whenever that may be. It will be unhurried time, the spirit unhurried, even though a watch lies before you.

It will be time with the Bible itself. If one has a Bible with good clear type, a copy pleasant to handle, and one isn't afraid to make notes in the margin, so much the better.

In that bit of time each day, multiplied by as many days as the calendar provides, the vision clears, the understanding is taught, the purpose stiffens, the judgment seasons and acquires balance, the spirit gentles, the heart becomes purer and hotter (the normal heart condition), the brain cooler, the feet steadier, the upreaching hand bolder, and the outreaching hand warmer. This is what *keeping in touch* means.

The continual *attitude* of mind and spirit comes instinctively under the sway of this new understanding. One goes the simple daily round with an unspoken prayer and an inner song.

This includes performing the endless daily tasks with a new spirit. They are done for him, as he did them in that Nazareth home and carpenter shop. The most ordinary things are done well because they are done under his eye.

A task may be monotonous, but never one's spirit. What would be drudgery becomes rhythm, because of the inner spirit. The ever-present One within, the song in your heart even when clouds gather, these sweeten the monotony.

When the unexpected comes, when the emergency suddenly looms, this quiet, steady attitude finds you ready. You are prepared. You hear the clear, quiet inner voice. You know instinctively what to do. Or you hold still and steady till you do know. This is what *keeping in touch* means.

Being *in touch* with Christ, and *keeping* in touch—this is the simple underlying condition for healing. Being in touch is the natural. Anything else is not human. It's an intrusion.

This simple natural touch with Christ means healthy, normal body. It means protection from that which threatens your health. It means the direct healing touch, if and when, disease actually gets in.

This is the first "how" of Christ's healing, the how of conditions, *getting and keeping in touch*. Sin broke and breaks the touch with Christ. We were started in touch back in Eden. We are born into this world in touch, at least, *creatively*. And that's no small thing.

The whole fabric of modern life, as it actually is, tends to the breaking of that touch. The willful doing of what we want to when we instinctively know we should do something else, this starts or strengthens the break.

Loss of touch means loss of strength, bodily strength. Disease and sickness and weakness in general, in some way, come through that break.

Coming to Christ, coming all the way, and staying—this opens the way for healing of every sort. When some day he comes back again, there will be the fullness of touch in his immediate presence. Then the last, lingering vestige of sin's break in our bodies will be gone. The body laid away in the dust, in a believing hope, will know the fullness of life again, as will those who are still living on that day.

The "How" of Method

The second "how" of healing is the *how of method*. What about the use of means? No question is more often asked in this connection, and there is the utmost confusion about the right answer.

When Christ was here, there was no science of healing. Men have always practiced a natural healing. The Jews have been noted for their skill in the use of herbs and other simple remedies, and in nursing. Luke was, in all probability, a physician.

Today we have far more knowledge of the human body, and of the effects of certain drugs and substances upon it. There has grown up through the years a storehouse of experience, wisdom, and skill. Properly used it is invaluable in discerning ailments and the best methods of treatment.

In spite of malpractice, faulty diagnosis, guesswork and experimentation, the unwise use of drugs, the commercialism, and an unwholesome professionalism, there is a human science of healing.

It is striking that some in that science today put greatest emphasis on the nonuse of drugs, on the sort and preparation and quantity of food, on the general habit of life, and on the mental attitude as the proper means of healing and avoiding illness.

Without doubt, there is the Christian physician, studious and conscientious, dispassionately abreast of the latest developments in his science, in real touch with Christ, and under the sway of the Holy Spirit, free from the pride of mere professionalism. Concerned above all else for the patient's recovery, with a simple faith in the present power of a living Christ, such a physician is aided by the Holy Spirit in discovering the real ailment and is used to minister relief and healing.

But you ask, "Where is such a physician?" I reply confidently that there have been such physicians and that there are still some, though one regrets their scarcity and prays most fervently that their number might be increased. This scarcity is, however, strictly in line with God's way of working. It makes greater the need of going directly to the great Physician.

Here is a quotation from a famous physician, taken from a standard religious journal:

"I believe that prayer does cure disease. Healing comes to some individuals directly through prayer, I am sure. I use it in my practice and rely on it today more often than on medicine. I believe that prayer is the contributing factor in the victory over disease.

"If I had no material means at hand, I should use prayer alone, with confidence that it would work the cure, if recovery were in conformity with God's will. And when prayer has thus been made a factor in recovery, I believe it is through direct action on the part of God."

The Seven Ways Healing May Come

It will help greatly to remember here that there are seven different ways in which healing may come to the diseased body: four natural, two supernatural, one a blend of the natural and supernatural.

There is a *natural healing without human cooperation*. The Creator has graciously put a healing power in the human body. If you cut your finger, instantly nature goes to work. The blood begins to coagulate and staunch the flow. That power within begins to make new tissue, to bring the two edges of the wound together, and to heal it completely.

There is this same *natural healing assisted by human cooperation*. A right mental attitude exerts enormous influence. The term "subjective mind" is used for certain mental faculties and processes.

The subjective mind, or the subjective functions of the mind, control the sensations and functions of the body. The imagination plays an incalculable part here. The objective mind or processes control the subjective mind as absolutely as the subjective mind controls the body.

Our knowledge, and reasoning, and deciding, and our insistent set-of-mind affect the imagination enormously. And this in turn actually controls in large measure bodily conditions.

Incidentally, this is the *process of faith at work,* a simple faith in Christ, in-breathed by his Holy Spirit.

The objective mind lays hold of Christ's promise and accepts unquestioningly the result as already assured. The subjective mind in obedience to that at once goes to work to produce the needed changes in the body.

In addition to this, as the need may be, Christ's supernatural touch exerts power directly on the body, also working through this purely natural process.

The thing to notice just now is that the whole mental attitude, both conscious and unconscious, affects enormously the free working of that natural healing power within every human body.

Then there is this *natural healing power assisted by expert knowledge and practiced skill.* Here is where the true physician comes in. The most a physician ever can do is to assist this natural healing power. The wise physician recognizes that he is merely nature's assistant. A physician's best work is in finding out what that natural power already knows—just what the trouble really is. Then real assistance can be given. Otherwise the physician is only a poor bungler. If one is sufficiently wise, and humble enough, and sometimes maybe unprofessional enough merely to be an assistant, so much the better.

When healing comes, what the assistant has done is the smaller part. That natural healing power has done the major portion, under the wonderful, unseen direct aid of a personal Physician.

My eye was quickly caught with the legend cut deep into the gray stone over a large hospital building near one of our largest eastern cities. It said: "Man tends; God mends." It is true. The actual healing is done by God. Any person's highest place is as an attendant.

Surely it would be scientific and wise and good common sense for the attendant physician to be in closest sympathetic touch with his Chief of Staff. What a tragic thing for the poor patient when we are not. This is the third way in which healing may come, the natural healing power within the body assisted by human skill.

The fourth way is a *natural healing, in spite of unwise bungling and lack of skill.* The human touch in this case puts a greater burden on the natural healing. And often the burden proves too much. The human touch is an interference. Nature is outdone, and the poor patient limps slowly along, or his life slips away.

There are two supernatural ways in which healing comes. One is *the direct supernatural touch of Christ,* in addition to anything that nature or human skill or both can do. This is the way this book is mainly concerned with.

The second is *the supernatural healing of the Devil.* It is a strange thing, and it is given separate treatment later in the book.

Last, there may be a blend of two or more of these. Four natural, two supernatural, and a blend of the natural and supernatural.

The Use of Means

Now we come directly to the question: what about the use of means? The answer is simple, and it is an answer that answers. There need be no evasion here, smothered up in foggy rhetoric.

The answer is this: *ask Christ.* Get in touch, if you are not already. Then, when the need comes, ask him. He will tell you. If you are in touch, and you will listen quietly you will hear his answer, clear and simple and positive.

Do you know the dominant law of the Christian life? It is obedience to the Holy Spirit's leading. This always takes first place. When there is any conflict, this law displaces all others.

But how shall one know just what his leading is? That question has already been answered when we talked about keeping in touch. Four things were named for keeping in touch with Christ, *act, purpose, habit, attitude.* That's the answer here. In that habitual touch we will know clearly just what the Holy Spirit would have us do. As we do what he tells us to, things will clear up for us.

Christ heals through means and the skilled human expert, sometimes. He heals without these, sometimes. He heals when the physician frankly confesses an inability to cure. Sometimes he heals by overcoming and counteracting the physician and the means used.

Ask him. He's there by your side, inside. He's intensely interested. He's eager to tell you what to do. In this he is a true physician, for he *advises.*

Remember it is His touch through the needed means that is effective. His own personal direct touch is more, much more, than the means or the expert human counsel that he knows your body may stand in need of.

The wise physician is an expert on the body, its functions and its needs. Your body may be needing something it isn't getting and needing it very badly.

Modern cooking, with some exceptions, is

washing out of the food vitamins and other nourishment that our bodies need for health and strength. Modern commercialism, for instance, is milling out of the wheat much of what the Creator put in it to meet our bodily needs.

No nation is better fed than ours yet, as a matter of sober fact, our bodies are being hurt, crippled, and starved for lack of needed nourishment. The Creator has put into the foods what our bodies need. We wash it out, or mill it out, or otherwise put or leave it out.

The physician may find our bodies ailing for lack of some element the food we eat should give, but doesn't. And if he is wise enough, he may help us live more in accord with the laws of physical health.

A simple, striking incident is told of Leo XIII. He was elected pope in his late sixties and was very frail in health. It is said that he was finally elected after a long contest because it was thought he could not live long. Then other plans could mature, and other ambitions among his electors could be achieved. So it was said. He outlived the entire College of Cardinals that elected him, finally dying in his ninety-fourth year, remarkable for his intellectual vigor and his masterful grip on his policies to the end.

He himself explained the human side of such a long life in spite of his extreme physical disabilities. He said he was not an expert in the knowledge of his body. He had a physician to advise him about the care of it.

He followed faithfully the regimen of food, exercise, sleep, and so on prescribed for him. Clearly, he must have had a wise and skilled physician. He attributed to this his remarkable mental vigor he maintained to the end of his long life.

We may be flagrantly disobeying some law of our bodies. Obedience is the universal law of all life. There can't be physical health without intelligent obedience to its laws.

Thoughtful, intelligent obedience to the laws of the body is strictly in accord with God's will for mankind. Obedience is the universal law of life. We may be flagrantly disobeying some law of our body, and there can't be bodily health without intelligent obedience to its laws.

Notice that in an emergency the supernatural as well as the natural swings into action. Life is full of emergencies.

I recall a friend who was suffering severely from some bodily ailment. She prayed repeatedly for healing, but it didn't come. And she wondered why. She was not conscious of any hindrance in her spiritual life. She had experienced healing by divine touch in answer to prayer more than once. She was in fellowship with a group of earnest, saintly people who taught that the use of medical means showed a lack of faith in Christ.

Puzzled, she went again to her knees in special prayer. The impression came, as distinct as a voice, to consult a certain physician. He was a Christian, who had formerly served her family and he was sympathetic with the teaching of healing by Christ's direct touch.

My friend hesitated to consult a physician because of the teaching of the group of Christians with whom she was in fellowship. But the idea to see this doctor persisted, and she knew it came in answer to her prayer.

The woman consulted the physician and in response to his questions told her story. He asked her what she ate. She said she could eat nothing but dry toast and tea. He told her these did not provide sufficient nutrition to her body in its present condition. He gave her no medicine, but simply directions for her diet and the care of her body. She followed his expert advice, continued praying, and she was soon well again.

Clearly, she needed advice to help her obey intelligently the law of her body. Through the advice, and the obedience, and Christ's touch, the healing came. Ask him. He'll tell you.

I recall one time when my back hurt me very much. I knew I had sinned in the matter of overwork. But I had repented and was trying to put my penitence into action. Still the nagging pain persisted.

I prayed for the healing touch. As clear as a bell, as quiet as the falling dew, the words were spoken into my inner ear, "Straighten up."

Years of travel, and of reading and writing on trains, had led to the habit of stooping. It was abnormal. My back was protesting. Pain is always a danger signal, graciously warning us. At once I began straightening up, and I have been straightening up ever since. The pain quickly left.

The Holy Spirit is practical. He wants to help. He helps our infirmities, of all sorts. Ask Christ. He'll tell you. And you'll hear if your ear is open, and your inner spirit quiet enough.

Do you remember the story of the healing of Hezekiah? (2 Kgs 20:1-18; Is 38:1-8, 21). In answer to Hezekiah's pleading prayer, Isaiah is sent with a message saying, "Take a cake of figs, and lay it for a plaster on the boil, and he will recover."

Then the supernatural backward shift of the shadow on the sun dial occurred as an indication that God was actually at work on Hezekiah's behalf. What an exquisite blend of the earthly and the divine, the natural and the supernatural!

Hezekiah's body needed something that human hands could do. His body also needed something that only God's touch could reach. The poultice did what it could. God's touch did what no poultice could have done. Both were used.

God loves nature's roads. But he unhesitatingly gives the more-than-natural touch when needed. Ask him. He'll tell you. Then be sure you give him the praise.

Sanity and Saintliness

There's a fellowship of saintly Christian people who, among other blessed truths, teach healing by Christ's direct touch. Their testimony and activity have been graciously owned and used by God throughout the United States and the foreign-mission world. They insist that no means be used. It is a common word among them that to consult a physician and to use medical means reveal a lack of faith.

One is reluctant to say a word that even seems critical of such people. Yet, clearly, such condemnation of medical means is not according to the teaching of scripture, nor the Holy Spirit's leading, nor God's general dealing with men, nor according to good sanctified common sense. The Holy Spirit's leading is the one touchstone of our actions.

One needs to avoid extremes. The sanity of the Holy Spirit awes. If one may say it with utmost reverence, the Holy Spirit is perfectly sane. There is no one so sane as the man under the control of the Holy Spirit. Saintliness and sanity naturally go together.

Faith Street is on the top of a hill. There are two roads slanting down on opposite sides, down to the lowlands and swamps. On one side is Doubt Street. The slant down is scarcely noticeable at first. And there are unseen traffic men always trying, by this means or that, to start you off that way, if ever so little at first.

On the opposite side of the hill is Peculiar Street. Its slant downward is also almost imperceptible at first. Still it's there. Peculiar Street has a large number of one-room bungalows. Many lovely, saintly people associate, all alone, each with himself, down there.

The only proper place to live is up on the top of the hill on Faith Street. The air is bracing there. Fogs and clouds are blown away. Indeed some object that the air is too sharp. It's a searching air, they say. And then, they say, it's such a steep slant up to the top. It pulls your strength so and takes your breath getting up.

But those who live there continually talk about the bracing quality of the atmosphere. The view is very clear and far and unobstructed. And there's a wondrous wind-harp on the top, whose soft rhythmic chordings refresh and strengthen.

Let us each one hire a moving van, if need be, and move up the steep slope to the top of the hill, and settle up on Faith Street, and refuse to be budged from our place by the insistent traffic man.

It is interesting to notice that it is entirely possible to be both sane and saintly. No one is so sane as one actually swayed by the Holy Spirit in his mental processes, as well as in the habit of his life.

Keeping in touch with Christ through the Bible, through bent knees, and through the regular recognition of his presence, and keeping in touch with other humans—this keeps one wholesomely sane. It seasons both spirit and mental judgment. Then, when any need arises, the first thing to do is to ask Christ for the healing touch, and to ask him what to do, if anything. He guides us in the use of our common sense. The man surrendered in heart and will is guided by the Holy Spirit in thinking through and in making decisions (Ps 25:9).

It ought to be commonplace that the first approach to all bodily ailments, slight or serious, should be prayer.

I remember a gentle-faced young mother, with two or three young children. She quietly said that as ailments arose with any of the children, she always prayed with them, simply and briefly. And she knew, she said, what a practical difference it made.

If it's a serious case, perhaps a chronic case, a bit of quiet time alone with Christ in scripture will help one get in touch afresh.

Ask Christ. Wait quietly for his answer. Cultivate the quiet inner spirit. Ask expectantly, remembering that it is his first will to heal. He is willing to heal, and, more, he is eager to heal. Reach out your hand and take all his pierced hand is reaching down to give.

A friend told me of having some serious physical trouble which seemed quite serious. She went to consult a trustworthy physician in a nearby city. After a thorough examination he diagnosed her as having breast cancer and strongly advised an operation. There was then in session in the city a gathering of physicians and surgeons. A certain eminent surgeon was in attendance. Arrangements could be made for the operation by this specialist.

But there was a restraint within, my friend said, a distinct restraint in her inner spirit. She did not agree. The physician warned against delay and plainly said it would be foolish not to do as he suggested at once. It was a peculiarly fortunate opportunity to have this visiting surgeon so immediately available, he said.

But the woman had prayed much before the consultation. The inner impression was clear. She returned home. And she prayed now with a clear knowledge of her serious need. She asked definitely for Christ's healing touch. And she told me that the lumps and the sense of distress gradually and completely left. This has been some years ago, and the trouble has not returned.

It was particularly interesting that she had no special contact at that time with those who taught healing. She is a thoughtful, quiet, earnest Christian woman, now past the prime of years, with no marked gift of leadership. Without any special prayer with others, she simply pled the promise of the Bible and asked for the healing, and it came.

Another friend had the beginning of what looked like cancer on her lower brow, plainly marked. The physician advised an operation and feared that without it she would lose sight in one eye. But she obeyed the inner restraint, not to have the operation.

My wife and I prayed with her, and at her request I later anointed her with oil, and again we prayed. The cancer never developed beyond the first stage, and after the anointing it gradually and completely left. There is now no mark to be seen.

Recently, a man whose home is in Texas told me of an experience of healing in his family. His six-year-old daughter had had a fever. The physician plainly revealed his anxiety and feared that her strength would not be sufficient. They thought she would not survive the night. It was a time of sorest distress.

The family was worn out with the watching and nursing, day and night, and the concern of spirit. The child's weakness was such that the family's usual evening prayers were held in the hallway with the door to the child's room left open. At the child's own request, a special prayer was made that Christ would heal her by his own direct touch. The family was greatly touched and impressed with her simple, strong faith.

She said to her father, "I'm going to be well now. Christ will heal me." She fell asleep with the words on her lips and a smile on her paled face. When the father and mother retired from the sick room one said to the other, "But suppose she isn't better in the morning; it'll be such a disappointment to her. What'll we do then?"

And the other replied, "But that isn't faith. Faith believes it will be as we asked." In the morning the child awoke with her temperature quite normal and speedily recovered her strength.

Let us live in simple, full touch with our living Christ. When any need may come, let us go to him. It is his eager will to advise us, and above all, to heal us, to his glory. For those we touch will know what a Christ Christ is. It will let them see his glory, that is, see the sort of a Savior he is.

FIVE

How Much Healing Can We Expect?

It is Christ's will that we be pure in heart, intelligent in understanding, well balanced in judgment, in the grip of a noble purpose, flamed by a strong passion, strong and well in body, and in touch in heart and in understanding with himself, where we can reach out and take all his pierced hands are now reaching down to give.

Healed but Limping

How far may Christ's power be expected to meet our bodily needs? We commonly say that there is no limit to his power to meet our spiritual needs. Is there a limit in our bodily needs? There is, of course, no limit to Christ's *power*. It seems to be a matter of his *willingness*, what he thinks it is best or wisest to do for us in this regard.

There's such a wide range of bodily ailments, running from a tension headache to organic heart trouble. Troubles that come from disturbed nervous conditions are more quickly affected by a changed mental attitude. Functional troubles are reckoned more susceptible to treatment than organic. Indeed organic troubles are usually ruled out.

Stress may bring on a serious palpitation of your heart. Peace from God relieves stress and takes care of the resultant problems. Some troubles are commonly classed as distinctly outside the range of healing, whether some system of mental suggestion, or Christ's own supernatural touch of power.

I recall running across a certain man in a western city. He was well known in Christian circles as a leader in mission work in New York City. He had made the journey west to get in touch with a Christian teacher of healing. And he told me that he had been healed of a rather serious trouble. But he had been lame for many years. As we parted he limped away. I looked after him. He was praising Christ for the healing of his body. But it had never occurred to him that this serious chronic lameness might have been healed too, nor apparently to the man who prayed with him. Was he right? Is there a limit in this regard?

Our next chapter emphasizes having the right mental attitude. A simple childlike trust in Christ affects one's habitual mental attitude. This in turn has an influence on all bodily conditions beyond what we can understand.

The Need, the Measure of Power

It is interesting to turn back and note the extent of Christ's healing in the days of the Gospel. The list of healings is composed primarily of incurable incorrigibles. A man blind from birth is included, with the possibility that his eyes had never fully matured or developed. One summary actually says that the maimed were made whole. There is only one meaning when that word "maimed" is used, whether the Greek or English word is examined. And that is, that a limb or arm or foot, or some other part that had been lost, was replaced by a new one. And then the last word in extremes is said in the raising of the dead, even Lazarus, dead four days.

The same sort of thing is repeated in Acts. The beggar in Jerusalem at the gate of the temple had been lame from birth. But the touch of Christ enables him to leap up and walk. There's an abundance of strength, where there had been none.

The man from Lystra had never walked. And, even here, there are the two dead people who are raised. There's Dorcas near the beginning of Acts, and there is the young man from Troas toward the end, when some might think that Christ's healing power was possibly waning.

There can be no question about how far healing was actually experienced in the days of the Gospel. *The need was the measure of the power.* The seriousness of the case didn't affect the power available. The degrees of disability varied. But there was no variance in the power at Christ's command, and in response to the disciples' Spirit-led actions. The power was always abundant and sufficient for the worst case. But what about now? How much healing may be expected today? Up to the limit of real need?

Ask Christ

There are two parts to the answer. The first is this: *ask Christ.* You can come into simple touch with him in which you can ask, and he will answer your question. That's an enormous advantage, to actually get in touch with Christ, who has all healing power.

Recall, if you will, what was said in the last chapter about getting in touch with Christ. Ask Christ. He has the power to heal. That is clear. He did have the love to heal when he was on earth. That's clear, also. He thought it wise to share his power through his followers in early church days.

Each one of us is a door. We are Christ's door, or we may be. We are his door into the whole circle where we live. He wants to go through us to others. His dealings with us are an acted-out plea to them. Through us he talks to others. The freer reign he has in our lives, the more he can touch others through us. We should eagerly, yet patiently, get into the sort of touch with Christ that allows him to give all that he wants. That means all we need.

Perhaps you are in that school we are to talk about soon. You need to learn a thing or two, maybe.

The thing we think we are needing may be withheld because there's something we are needing more. We may not know about that other need. It may require a radical change to recognize that other need, and more radical yet to be willing to fulfill it, with all it involves.

It may be that the Devil is hindering. There is no bit of teaching he more bitterly hates, and more stubbornly fights against, than that of bodily healing by Christ's supernatural touch. Those who are in places of leadership, or who have the personal gift of leadership, are yet more bitterly opposed than those otherwise placed or gifted.

One often has to insist in spite of bitter opposition. The thing is to be certain of the Holy Spirit's leading, and then to insist on having all he has for you.

Ask Christ your question. And remember, as

you ask, his *first* will for you. It includes full bodily health and vigor, to his glory. That's the first half of the answer.

God's Giving: Our Taking

The second part goes a little deeper. It is this: Christ's *giving* is dependent on our *taking*. You can't give to someone with a tightly shut fist. Christ can't.

There's a striking little word on Christ's lips in his betrayal night talk (Jn 15:16). He and his inner group are walking under the full moon, past Herod's temple with its beautiful brass grapevine.

Christ says, "You did not choose me, but I chose you." They did choose him as a Savior. He chose them for the bit of service they were to do.

"And I appointed you," he goes on, "that you should go and bear fruit." The fruit was the life, the inner life where all service is rooted. "And that your fruit shall abide." Not green, gnarled fruit, but full-grown, luscious, juicy fruit. He means us to live a life matured and ripened in its spiritual experiences.

"That whatsoever you shall ask." Note that prayer, like service, grows out of the life. The life in touch prays, and can pray, and can pray the prayer that calls forth Christ's power *to the full*.

"Whatsoever you shall ask the Father in my

name, He *may* give it you." The striking word is that word "may." It is not *shall* this time, but *may*. Every other time the word used in this connection is shall; this time it is may. "Shall" means his willingness to do; it means his purpose. "May" means our cooperation with him. "Shall" is his side, "may" is ours: our asking makes it possible for God to give. We give him the open channel. God needs an open hand and that means an open life.

Christ's giving is always dependent on our taking. But we are such beggarly takers. No human hand has ever yet reached up to take as much as Christ's pierced hand is reaching down to give. For the taking must be on a level with the giving. It means that touch where we want to receive what he wants to give. He leads us. We follow.

We talk much about God's sovereignty, without understanding much about just what it means. We don't talk so much about man's sovereignty. Practically, God's sovereignty means that ultimately, through the tangled-up network of human wills, God's love-plan for mankind will work out fully. Yet it will be without infringing on any man's free choice and action.

Man's sovereignty, as planned by God, means that everything we have and get and do is through our own choice. God's sovereignty waits on man's sovereignty, his purposes on our glad cooperation. Some day these two will run side by side. Man's sovereignty will be deliberately merged in God's. His love will win our choice.

But, just now, the point to emphasize is this: the most important aspect of life is our taking. We may have, out of Christ's down-stretched hand, all we *can* take, and then all we actually *will* take, and *do* take.

It's a three-sided transaction. Christ reaches down to give all we need, without any limit or restriction. We reach up and take out of his hand. The Devil reaches over to keep us from taking out of Christ's hand. He tries to keep our hands, Christ's hand and mine, out of touch, if possible. He clouds the air so we don't see straight in our reaching. He tries to teeter our reaching hands, this way and that, or to make them not reach up far enough. He does his best to tire us, to wear us out, so we'll quit the reaching. When he slips in one area, he starts in afresh in another.

The Limit of Our Consent

Paul writes a verse that fits in here. It says that all power needed by any one (in touch with Christ) is already within himself. It is a matter of letting this power that is within actually meet the need. The need you feel so keenly and the power to meet that need are close neighbors. You have both. It's a matter of the two getting together.

The passage is from an address to the Ephesians, the people among whom Paul had a remarkable healing ministry. It becomes the more striking because the particular thing discussed in this letter is the power of God *at our disposal* to meet our need.

There's a threefold standard or measure of that power: the raising of Christ when he was dead (Eph 1:18-22), the making of a new man inside one dead in sin (Eph 2:1-10), and the changing of bitterest enemies into dearest friends (Eph 2:11-22). Only a high standard of power could do such things!

Paul says we may expect *that* power, which is now within us, to meet any need for us today up to that measure or limit. That covers what we are talking about just now, and more.

The striking passage comes at the end of chapter three (Eph 3:16-20). In simple language Paul says that the Holy Spirit *is* power. He in himself is all the power of God. He is now inside each of us. He comes in through the opened door of faith. He reproduces Christ's own character in us, so far as we let him have his way. He fills our hearts with that tender, strong passion, the love of Christ.

Paul sums it up in this: "Unto Him who is able to do exceeding abundantly above all we ask or think, according to the power that worketh in us." That is to say, he is able to do, not simply what we ask, but also what we are *thinking* about and wishing he would do.

Then Paul piles things up in a rare way. He is able to do *above* that, then *abundantly* above that, then *exceeding* abundantly above that.

The one outstanding characteristic of this power is *love*. It is a power of love. He can and he will. Love controls the power. That surely answers our question.

The measure, limit, or extent up to which we may expect this power is put in these words, *"according to the power that worketh in us."* That means up to the measure of that power working in us.

Of course, the power itself is without any limit. But the Holy Spirit always works with our consent. He does only as much as we let him do. Everything he does is as we are willing. So the limit of the working is *the limit of our consent.* He will do all we let him.

As we let Him work *in* us all he wants to, he works *for* us all we need. If we let him work character *in* us (Christ's character), he's free to work bodily healing *for* us.

If we let him work out his fruit *in* us—love, joy, peace, long-suffering, gentleness, goodness, meekness, faithfulness, self-mastery—then He is free to work out *for* us the healing our bodies need and our circumstances, too.

Fruit-growing is a gradual thing, it involves

seed-sowing, pruning, sun and rain, dew and air, spraying for hurtful insects, then bud and blossom, the beginning of the fruit, and its gradual growth as a juicy, luscious, full-sized fruit. It's gradual. All growth is. One must be patient and steady, very steady. But sometimes growth is surprisingly quick when it is the fruit the Holy Spirit bears in the soil of our character.

Nine Things about Taking

How much can we expect Christ's healing? We *may* have all we *can* take. And then all we *do* take. But notice a few simple yet radical things about the taking. The taking must be in Christ's name, pleading his blood. The Devil yields only to whom he must. And he must to Christ.

The taking must be by one in touch of heart with Christ. The Devil laughs at any one else.

The taking must be in the utmost humility. Our sins cost Christ so much suffering; whatever we take has been bought for us with his blood.

The taking must be definite. The Devil yields only *what* he must. The taking must be persistent. The Devil yields only *when* he must. He's a sly, deceitful, toughened fighter by strategy as well as by ugly force.

The taking must be as the Holy Spirit guides. The touchstone of all prayer is the Holy Spirit's guidance. He puts the prayer to be prayed into one's heart. No mere asking for something because of someone else's experience will do. That experience may be blessed. But there must be one's own direct leading, over the open Bible, on the bent knee.

The taking must be *with the life*. No mere church membership, and activity and giving, and the like, will do. No simple taking of the sacred bread and the holy cup will answer here. These may all be very blessed. But the taking must be with the very life. One finds that it is only the life actually lived for Christ, by his grace, that can reach up and take to the full what his blood has redeemed.

Then you take only as much as you *can* take. The power to take varies with different persons, and even at various times with the same person. It all depends on one's personal touch with Christ.

You take only as much as you actually *do* take. As a rule, the conception of *how much* you may take varies. It varies with circumstances and with one's mood. The Spirit's leading is the decisive thing.

But it is Christ's first will that we shall be made strong and well in our bodies *up to the limit of our need*. He is by your side, now, eagerly waiting to give. Giving won't make him any poorer, only gladder.

James Moore Hickson is a Church-of-England

layman with a remarkable healing ministry. One day I asked him to tell me the most notable instances of healing of which he knew personally. And he told me of two that I want to relate here.

Mr. Hickson had gone to visit a woman in her home in the Midlands in England. She had been bedridden for years with rheumatoid arthritis, an incurable disease that affects the joints of the body. In this case the joints were locked up or rigid. The woman had not been able to move herself for several years.

Mr. Hickson prayed for her healing. That evening she moved herself, for the first time in years. Her husband wrote that the next morning she rose from the bed, dressed herself, and went about the house, as in earlier years.

The second incident concerned a twelve-year-old boy with a club foot from birth. He was brought to a church where a healing mission was being conducted. He came up to the front of the church with his attendant, wearing an iron brace to help him walk.

As Mr. Hickson saw the boy in front of him, he said to himself involuntarily, "Oh! this is a *deformity*!" His thought was that this was not a disease, but a much different and much more difficult case to handle.

In telling me the story, Mr. Hickson said that instantly that quiet inner voice said, "Who is doing this? You or I?"

He said in his heart, "Forgive me, Lord," and aloud he said to the attendant, "Take off the irons." He took the boy's foot in his hands and said a simple prayer, as was his custom.

The next day the boy was brought again. There was some improvement in the foot. Again he prayed, and the boy's foot gradually became normal.

How far may Christ's healing be expected? We may have all we can take, as his Spirit guides our taking.

Blessed Christ, solitary God-Man, who lived a full life of human experience, and then died as none other did nor could nor can, and then lived again, and still lives, and some day will finish up the end of your task on earth, help me now to reach out and up and take out of your pierced hand all you have for me, to your glory among my fellows.

I ask it on the ground of your blood shed for me, and your Word pledged to me. Amen.

SIX

The Human Side of Healing and Health

It is Christ's will that we be pure in heart and motive and life, truly human in character up to the level of his humanness, fired by a noble passion, in the grip of a worthy purpose, in warm touch with himself and with our fellows, and strong and vigorous in all our bodily functions.

Health or Healing?

Health is more than healing. It calls for more of the Creator's power. It means more to a man. And it will be the means of greater spiritual blessing if things are as they were meant to be.

The task of keeping people in health is immeasurably greater than healing all who need healing, even if they would all come for healing.

Christ is greatest in the unrecognized power he is expending on us all the time. All this power has the mark of Calvary upon it. It is all red-tinged.

Health means rhythm, the smooth working of all parts together. Disease is a break in that rhythm. Rhythm is ease. A break in the rhythm means absence of ease, dis-ease, of some sort. When there is full rhythm within your body and with your fellows and with Christ and with nature, there is fullness of life flowing in and flooding out. But there is a break, a bad break in the rhythm of life, within and without and above. Within we call it disease, without friction and strife and war. Above we call it sin.

In spite of the break, Christ continues his touch of creative power on all life, giving health and strength. This touch becomes less as we turn from him.

Fullness of life comes only as we let him do and give all he wants to. The added touch, healing, is given where the way is open to him.

The gift of health and strength is natural healing; healing includes the supernatural in addition to the natural. The first is for all, the second is for those needing it and those who will come to where Christ can give it.

Being *kept in health* is better than being healed. Then healing isn't needed. It reflects a greater obedience in the taking from Christ's hand, day by day, all that we need. And it costs Christ more in the continual giving out of power.

Christ's creative power through natural channels is commonplace, blessedly commonplace. It is everywhere. It is in every one, without exception.

His supernatural power is exceptional. Where his natural power is most at work, there is less need of the supernatural.

But that break of sin is so evident, that there is a constant need of the supernatural. And there would be far more of the supernatural if more men and women were open to Christ. For Christ will do anything and everything to overcome the break of sin. He came that we might have life, and have it in uncommon measure.

There is the divine side of health and healing, and there is the human side. The two intermingle so continually that it's difficult to talk about the one without touching on the other. But, just now, we want to talk a little about the human side.

Living in touch with Christ's natural laws of life and in direct touch with him, where health is common, and healing is not needed, *this,* is the highest level of living.

It is striking to find two distinct trails in the Old Testament, a healing trail and a health trail. The two run side by side. The health trail is greater in the space it takes up and in the emphasis put upon it. This is an interesting point because the way God dealt with Israel in the Old Testament is similar to the way he deals with the modern church.

We traced partially, in chapter two, the healing

trail in the Old Testament. It was a trail of teaching and of healing. We saw God's healing touch and how it was used as a plea to pull the Israelites up to the higher level of life.

The Jewish Health Trail

Side by side with the supernatural trail goes this other trail, longer, broader, more marked. It is a teaching about health in which God repeatedly instructs the Israelites and calls them to obedience.

Some of the Lord's commands may seem simple and commonplace. But careful attention and obedience to detail brings about perfection. And nothing is too common if its practice means physical vigor. Physical vigor affects mental alertness and spiritual attainment.

Particular stress is put on *food*. God carefully teaches the Israelites what they should and should not eat (Lv 11:1-23). And Moses repeats the Lord's teachings in the last series of talks given at the plains of Moab (Dt 14:3-21). This would cultivate a thoughtfulness about food. A hygienic principle underlies all the instructions and restrictions.

The Israelites were an agricultural people, with small exporting facilities, and so the fruits of trees and soil would naturally form a large portion of their daily diet. *Physical exercise* was also stressed. There was plenty of work to be done in connection with the cultivation of fields, orchards, vineyards, and common gardening.

Every Hebrew had some fixed occupation, and every one shared in the daily tasks, indoors and out.

Particular attention was also given to *rest*, to relaxation. God's teaching brought about a rare balance between work and rest.

Four distinct items make up the rest or relaxation program that Moses was careful to mark out for the Israelites, at God's direction. One day in seven was to be kept, sacred from toil, for the resting of the body. Three times a year the Israelites put aside their usual occupations to celebrate special events. These were the Passover, the Feast of the First-fruits, and the Harvesthome Festival. Each lasted for seven days.

The men were to go up to Jerusalem to these feasts. Including travel, it must have meant a tenday holiday for most of them.

Every seven years the Israelites let the land lie fallow. Modern farmers might well note this. The land enriched itself. The land rested, and of course the people rested.

Every fiftieth year was the time of special jubilation, following the plan of the seventh year. The average man would live through at least two of these jubilee years.

Then, of course, rest was taken every night.

There was the daily alternation of rest and work. Nature itself provides for more sleep in winter and less in summer. The Israelites followed nature more closely than we do.

All told, God taught the Israelites to rest one day out of every seven, three special times each year, one year out of every seven, and an extra year in every fifty years.

It was a remarkable program. Yet the fact that it was provided by Moses, at God's direction, is suggestive.

Physical exercise, and time for the mind to store up and meditate, time for social recreation and enjoyment, time for worship, all this becomes of greatest interest for the maintenance of personal health.

Particular directions were also given about *the ablutions,* the frequent bathing by the priests. And the priests were the practical rulers of the people. Through the centuries, the priesthood was the fixed system of national administration. Priests were the leaders, and what the leaders did, the people did.

Directions were given for special bathing in connection with sanitary and quarantine codes. They were a bathing people. Cleanliness of person was a fixed habit.

Community *sanitation* regulations covered the individual tents and the whole encampment in the wilderness, and afterward in Canaan. The *quarantine* regulations were explicit and rigid, they involved inspection by experts, isolation, and segregation. The strictest watch was constantly kept on the people's health, on all suspicious cases, and on the diseased. Quarantine is worthless unless rigid, and rigidly enforced.

Of course, the inflexible law of *circumcision* was rooted in the physical. Apart from other significance, it was a hygienic regulation. It was part of their scheme for cleanliness and provision against infection.

Also, the Hebrews were essentially *an out-of-doors people*. They lived in God's open air. They spent 400 years in Egypt. Egypt was an open-air country characteristically, and is to this day. The absence of rain, the dryness of the air, and its rare tonic qualities were marked features. They spent forty years in the open air of the wilderness, where most of them probably slept outside.

Moses himself was used to this open-air life because of his sheep-tending years in Midian, as well as his earlier years in Egypt and in the wilderness.

Another teaching that strengthened the health of the Hebrews centered on the *land laws*. The scheme of inheritance, the reversion of land to the original owner every fifty years eased anxieties regarding the future. Fear of the future makes a shorter road to the graveyard.

These eight items were part of the Israelites'

national health program through the centuries. These include food, work or exercise, rest and relaxation and play, personal cleanliness, community sanitary measures, quarantine against disease, open-air living, and a measure of contentment about the future.

This is the trail of health that runs all through the pages of the Old Testament, and which clearly ran all through the physical life of the Jews.

Inheritance persists. The Jews have suffered persecutions, hardships, and privations, that would have killed off any ordinary people. Plainly, they are not ordinary people. Their health program certainly was not ordinary. It was rather extraordinary.

The health trail runs side by side with that blessed healing trail. It puts a remarkable emphasis on the human side of health and healing. It was planned by God and may serve as a personal model for us.

The Eden Health Model

The Old Testament describes another model of life before it describes the model of the Hebrew nation. It comes in before the break of sin had set things askew. It's the model of the true, full human, the human as yet unhurt by sin. It's the Adam-and-Eve-in-Eden model.

It is put at the opening of the Bible because it is God's ideal of human life.

Of course, I am a little old-fashioned about man's start on this earth. Other teaching has so clouded the air that it's quite refreshing to turn back to God's own picture. I am rather fond of some old-fashioned things, water, open air, fresh fruit, natural wheat, the Bible, and the like.

Adam was made the true, full, normal human, by direct act of God. He stood at the highest point of maturity physically, mentally, and spiritually. He knew civilization at its hightest, in miniature. For civilization does not consist in the culture which the Greeks had, nor the highly organized life of the Roman, nor the organized complexity of modern times.

Civilization involves morals. Civilization means harmonious life in contact with others. The essential is moral ideals and moral conduct. So far as any civilization lacks these, it is less than real civilization.

Look at God's picture, his model in Eden. It is delightfully simple, but never crude, and certainly not savage. Here is a human, fresh from the hand of God. He is on terms of intimacy with God. They talk and walk and are busily occupied with their work together. This man has an intimate, congenial human friend at his side sharing all his life. He has a daily occupation, caring for a garden. He has before him a great inspiring task, subduing the whole earth. There is the immediate and the distant, the near and the far, something for hands and something for mind.

He lived in the open air, sleeping as well as working and resting there. The second day he lived was marked as a day of rest. He had a daily task, work and exercise combined. He had a fruit diet. His food was all sun-cooked. He had pure water to drink. There was running water to bathe in.

Is it not an attractive picture? Certainly it would be a step *up* to return back to that old Eden standard of civilization and culture and life.

There is the plain intimation, too, that this first man's bodily vigor hinged on his keeping in touch with his friendly Companion, God.

Do you remember the day Adam and Eve were standing under that tree of opportunity? Through choosing not to eat of it as God wished him not to do, deciding to choose God's choice, Adam would be stepping into a still closer intimacy with God. The highest good can come only through choice.

God gave a gentle but very plain word of warning about that tree. Adam *could* misuse the opportunity it gave him. He *could* break friendship with God if he chose.

This is the word of warning, "For in the day

that thou eatest thereof, dying, thou shalt die"
(Gn 2:17, paraphrase). The dying would come
automatically through the break. The moment he
ate was the beginning. The process went on for
years. The actual bodily death didn't come till
long years after.

Now, that intimation naturally includes the
reverse, i.e., if you keep in touch with me, by your
own voluntary choice, *living, you shall live.*

This involves a similar movement in the opposite direction, a beginning, a process, a final
result. Choosing God's way would bring him yet
closer to God. That would be the beginning of a
new life by Adam's own choice. And it would
grow from less to more until a fullness of life
would come.

Contact with God is the basis of full life,
bodily, mental, of the spiritually.

The other word for touch is obedience. Obedience is a music word. It means the rhythm of
God's will and a man's will. No sweeter music was
ever made on earth or heard in heaven.

All this, notice, has to do with the human side
of health. This early model gives God's own
thought of the true, fully natural human man, as
he planned him. This Eden idea says, in effect,
that a person should have a noble passion, human
companionship, a daily task, and an outreaching
purpose that calls for unselfish giving. His

immediate bodily needs are open air, simple food, the exercise of a daily task, a time of rest, and running water near by.

This first man's passion was for his Friend, to please him, to carry out his plan. By his side was Eve his complemental self, his one, closest human friend with whom all his life was shared.

He lived in a garden of trees and flowers and all growing things to care for, and the cultivation of the whole earth was entrusted to man to think about and plan for.

The Christian and the True Human

The Christian life is, simply, the true human life. Sin caused the break. Christ mends the break. He renews and restores man. It is natural for us to live the true, full, Christian life.

Anything that isn't really Christian isn't human. It's lower. It's less than human, or a distortion. Sin and selfishness are lower than obedience and honesty. They hurt the true human. They hurt our health and strength. The true Christian life is the real key to health and to healing where healing is needed. The emphasis, of course, is on that word "true."

We are so used to the cheapened, thinned-out meanings, being "saved" from hell and into heaven, belonging to a church with some giving of money and maybe service, as happens to suit one's ideas; this seems the sum total ofttimes.

Christianity is viewed as a sort of insurance policy. The chief thing is keeping up the premiums. It's a sort of immunity bath, a quarantine measure. Sometimes it is the ticket of admission into certain social circles. Such Christianity has no ethical quality to it. It never hurts anybody's conscience, nor changes anyone's habits.

Of course, in the simple, true meaning the Christian life is a tender passion burning deep and then deeper. It's a purpose gripping all one's powers. It means, on the inner side, spiritual fellowship with the Man that died; on the outer side, a warm upright human touch with one's fellows. It is very simple. Some of the simplest, homeliest folks, as well as some of the most scholarly and cultured, understand all this. They live it.

Christ enriches everything he touches. The Devil vulgarizes everything he can lay his hands on. Christ makes the most common thing hallowed. The Devil makes the purest, the hallowed things, vulgarly common and cheap.

The Devil puts the evil touch into man's life, sometimes foul, sometimes cultured, always evil. Christ restores the hurt human up to the true human level. Calvary neutralizes the Devil's power, and restores and enriches the Eden ideal. The new Eden has the passion of sacrificial love in it.

The simple, real Christian life is the key to health and to healing. This is the human side of both.

One's Mental Attitude

Two things will grow up in a true and simple Christian life: a right mental attitude and an intelligent obedience of the laws of health. These are the two things to be emphasized in this chapter.

Let us talk first about that *right mental attitude*. I do not mean that you are simply to try to have a right mental attitude. That becomes incidental. The emphasis is on something else. The right attitude comes naturally out of that something else.

Look to Christ. He died for you. He has won the love of your heart. Trust him. Believe him. Accept what he says in the Bible. Follow where he plainly leads. All this is faith. It is thinking about him.

Consider who he is, how he loved and loves, what he did, his plans for you, and his promises to you. He is living today, and he is intensely interested in you, with personal solicitude for your personal need, and with a plan for your life.

This is what faith means; not thinking about your faith, but thinking about *him*. It isn't looking *in*; it's looking *up*—to *him*.

Once this becomes a growing habit, it will affect your mental attitude. Your plans and problems, your difficulties and perplexities, your personal habits and temptation, all will instinctively be affected by this mental attitude.

Christ will loom up in your mind as the biggest thing in all your life. You will get into the habit of connecting everything with him. And *that mental attitude will vitally and radically affect your body*.

The worst enemy we all have (outside of the Devil himself) is fear. There are three kinds of fear. The fear that is reverence grows out of love, and is good. The fear that is caution grows out of the presence or possibility of danger, and is only good. The fear that is afraid of something or someone, a dread, a slavish fear, is bad and injures one's body.

Fear may grow out of ignorance. Often it is a result of overwrought nerves. It exerts an incalculable influence on one's bodily condition. It controls the imagination, and the imagination controls the body. Some injuries are imaginary and have no existence at all except in the mind. Other ailments are the result of the imagination's influence on the body. And then there are ailments originating otherwise.

Job says, "I feared a fear and it came upon me" (Jb 3:25, paraphrase). His sense of dread acted so on his imagination that it actually produced in his body the thing he feared.

Faith Runs Fear Out-of-Doors

A simple childlike trust in Christ drives that spirit of dread and fear far away (1 Jn 4:18). It changes radically one's mental attitude. The imagination is radically affected and begins at once to work changes in the body.

It works in three ways. It will actually remove imaginary ills, and also those ills resulting from a tortured imagination. It will work toward changing bodily conditions, healing where there has been weakness and disease. It will tend steadily toward keeping one in prime condition, in full vigor and strength. It will ward off disease, threatening by contact.

A new mental attitude particularly affects one's nerves. It relaxes tense nerves. Tension is responsible for many bodily ailments. Normal relaxation removes a long list of bodily ills.

What I am speaking of now is on the purely natural level. The right touch with Christ affects the mental attitude. And the mental attitude largely controls the functions and sensations of the body.

I heard the following story from a reliable source about a famous Philadelphia physician. The woman who consulted him told the story.

She had a nervous temperament, and her numerous troubles had worried her to such a degree that they affected her health and even threatened to affect her mental balance.

The eminent doctor listened, and then quietly told her to read her Bible an hour a day and report again in a month. She was indignant. He gently insisted. Reflection led her conscientiously to do as he advised. The change was most marked. On reporting again, she asked the physician how he had known just what she needed.

The famous physician turned to a worn, marked Bible lying open on his table, and said with deep earnestness, "Madam, if I were to omit my daily reading of this Book I would lose my greatest source of strength and skill.

"I never go to an operation, or a distressing case, without reading my Bible. Your case called, not for medicine, but for a source of peace and strength outside your own mind. I gave you my own prescription. I knew it would cure."

Turning your thought toward Christ fills you with the conception of his reality, his love, his power. Time daily spent over the Bible, reaching through to Christ, brooding thoughtfully about him, all this brings that attitude of heart and mind commonly called *faith*.

It fills your heart with love, love for him. And love, this drawing of yourself out tenderly toward him, this casts that slavish fear out.

You don't try to turn it out. You are thinking of Christ. He draws your heart out to him. You resist the fear. It goes. The love drives it out.

Note that simple faith in Christ does two things. It *releases that natural creative healing power* within your body. That power swings into action. Its power is beyond calculation. At least, nobody has yet calculated it fully or adequately.

It does a second thing. It *opens the way for any direct supernatural touch* needed in addition to that natural, creative healing power. It was in the days of his wisdom that Solomon said, "A tranquil heart is the life of the flesh" (Prv 14:30). The *right mental attitude* which comes as a *natural result* of a simple, true faith in Christ.

The Body—Master or Servant?

What is the second thing that will mark the true Christian? Shall I say obedience to God's laws? That is only part of the answer. The full answer includes obedience to Christ *in everything*, and this includes *the common laws of health*.

Now, some Christians will begin to think that this is dropping to a rather low level. "The laws of our *body*!" you say.

The truth is it is climbing up a bit for most of us. Oh, yes, I know you say you would gladly sacrifice bodily comforts and strength for Christ's sake. And you mean it.

But you need to be on your guard lest you disregard the law of your body *for your own sake*, because of what you prefer, or don't prefer.

This may deprive Christ of the messenger he needs. You may be giving him a poorer crippled service when you needn't. And it may be in an emergency when your poorer service, your failure, slows up his plans.

For *Christ's sake,* in the thick of the emergency of life, the true Christian seeks to make his body the strongest possible, the most disciplined channel through which Christ's power may flow. This is done through a thoughtful obedience to its laws.

This is keeping "the body under," under the control of that Christ passion. Disobeying its law, carelessness, not-thinking, all help give your body the upper hand.

Christ has been robbed of the needed service of many saintly children of his, through unconscious, thoughtless disregard of the body.

The touchstone of the Christian life is the same as the touchstone of the true human life, *obedience.* But obedience is not a matter of doing or not doing certain things.

It's on a higher level than that. It's doing as a certain One wants or would prefer. Not "things," but "a Person" holds your eye. It means getting or keeping in better shape for the errand he has sent you on.

The thing that seems small or trivial in itself is now thought seriously about. In this way you can be a truer Christian in your conduct, better fitted for what God wants done, and more serviceable to others.

It's astonishing how common indifference to, and disobedience of, the rhythmic laws of health, is among not only good, but really saintly, people. Such disobedience or indifference or carelessness in other matters would rule a man out of life. It would make him a forced exile. He couldn't keep a bank account without careful obedience to the laws of the bank. He couldn't run an automobile, nor be a student in any sort of college or school, nor run a successful business, nor move in polite society, nor be a member of a club. Obedience to law (a recognized agreed-upon sequence of action) is the commonplace of all intercourse.

This principle is even more crucial when it concerns a Christian, especially when it concerns his body. For the Christian aims to live the truly ideal life in a practical way, for *Christ's sake,* as well as for his own.

His body is the fine tool he works with. He will keep this tool in the best possible shape all the time for the sake of the work it does.

The true Christian takes pains to learn about the body and to think about its need, so that he can be free of the body, free to do his work.

Obedience means intelligence, being informed, becoming skilled. So the habit of a wise obedience is formed, and one is strong and free.

One thinks about the body in order to forget it and get on with the work.

It is striking that scripture gives principles for everything we need. It gives two models for the bodily life. The earliest is Adam in Eden before the serpent got in. The second is the model of God's messenger nation, Israel. It is much fuller and more explicit, because the serpent had gotten in.

Recalling these two models, there are some six things that thoughtful Christians will think about, so they needn't think about them when absorbed in their work. These are the six things: food, air, exercise, sleep, cleansing, and posture.

Six or Sick?

The body needs *food*. How much does it need? Enough to keep it strong and fit, *and* no more. Many of us overeat. Much of our strength is taken up in digesting food that tastes good, but adds nothing to our strength. Indeed it takes from strength and makes us less fit.

The sense of taste should not decide what we eat. It has its important place. But knowledge of food, the sense of taste, and keeping fit for one's work, these together should decide.

The body needs food of the sort that will keep it in the best fighting shape. One naturally believes that the Creator thought about our bodily needs in the provision he made. For instance, wheat has in it numerous substances that our bodies need. If commercialism takes most of that nourishment out, so that the whitened product can be stored without spoiling and loss of money, one naturally avoids such a product. Eating such foods robs the body of the nutrition it *must* have for health and vigor.

If the way the food is cooked washes most of the nutrients away, clearly the body suffers. A man may be partially starved, even with a loaded table, and a full stomach.

Eating the right proportion of food is important. In Eden, Adam reached *up* for his food. He had a fruit and nut diet. It was all sun-cooked. After the flood, Noah reached down as well as up. He added the things that grew under and close to the soil. And he added animal food.

This suggests that the original diet was a fruit and nut diet. But all life has greatly changed. It is no longer normal as it was in Eden. What is absolutely best (outside of morals), is very often not best under certain circumstances. And this change affects our bodies and their need.

Life is more than food, much more. The thoughtful person comes to know that a radical change takes place in the body after it has fully matured. The building stage is past. While growing, it required certain foods that go to building the body up to its maturity. Now, food is taken simply to repair the waste of the day's work.

Eating more than that adds excessive weight, which itself is a diseased condition, and leads to other diseased conditions. Insurance companies take weight into account to modify their standard tables. Money sharpens the need to look closely at this element of fitness.

The thoughtful person comes to find that after a certain age a smaller quantity, a lessening or omitting of the heavier foods (meats, eggs, and the like), actually adds to the physical and mental vigor.

The Christian takes this into account because it affects his Christian character and usefulness to our Master.

The common diet of some nations consists mainly of meat, potatoes, and white bread and excludes green leafy vegetables and juicy fruits. Yet dietary experts insist on the necessity of a balanced diet, and especially on a lessening of the heavier foods and an increase of the lighter, in the middle life and after.

The thoughtful Christian thinks about these things in a sober, sane, sensible way, adjusting habits and keeping the body under control. So the Christian is freer and stronger for his life task.

I recall an unusually saintly man of New York City, a great Christian leader, much blessed in service as a layman. He had a serious illness. He taught about healing and had experienced it. But now it didn't come, and he wondered why. He held his spirit quiet and waited on God in prayer, to know if there was anything hindering his healing.

The answer came. It was in a single word. It was the name of a certain kind of meat of which he was rather fond. Apparently, he had been eating it to excess. The Holy Spirit teaches simple things, if we are willing to listen.

Man is *an open-air being*. Our abnormal modern life, called (or miscalled) civilization, has made him an indoor animal. One of the most prevalent diseases in many countries of the world, tuberculosis of the lungs, is an indoor disease.

There is no question that the common indoor habit both weakens and shortens life. As things actually are we can't live a wholly outdoors life. But the nearer we can come to it the nearer we are to the true full normal human. And no words are adequate to tell the physical blessedness of sleep in the open air. There is nothing that so rebuilds and cushions one's nerves.

Our bodies also need *exercise*. Many of us have to work with our bodily strength for a living, and that gives a certain amount of exercise, though modern life is apt to make it insufficient.

Watch your baby on the floor twisting and stretching strenuously, pulling and turning. That's its exercise. That helps the baby digest the food and keep healthy and grow.

A good form of exercise is walking—an easy swinging walk, with soft shoes, and loose-fitting clothing, head up, chest out, and arms swinging. Graduated walking, beginning with little and increasing gradually, until several miles are easily done, will work wonders simply developing and maintaining bodily strength.

One can say that the true Christian walks for health, for *Jesus' sake*. The healthy Christian can be of better service to his fellows, and find the zest, the sheer zest, of being alive.

If the editor of a religious paper finds that an hour's easy walk to his desk or away from it, clears his brain, and steadies his nerves, and sharpens his sentences, and makes clearer and simpler his pen-preaching and teaching, *if* so, he will never miss that walk.

Exercise should include everything from toes to hair, and out to fingertips. Ten minutes, morning and night, in the open air or at an open window, doing a simple series of stretching exercises, regardless of age, is a necessity for vigorous health. In this way the body is stretched, thoroughly stretched from head to foot. Watch the baby. He is a good teacher of how to do it. Or the cat after a nap.

In general, *sleep* requires little effort. Some people sleep too much, while others ought to sleep more. Sleep can be a confession of faith, when your body needs it but anxiety keeps you awake.

The thoughtful Christian follows a regular sleeping pattern. One should plan for enough sleep, sometimes foregoing lesser obligations in order to get enough sound, deep, refreshing sleep. Sleep renews the strength.

If the mother finds that a half-hour's lying down in a quiet room in daytime, whether sleep comes or not, makes her more patient with the children and gives her better self-control in the home, she will prayerfully plan for it. So she is a truer Christian mother, and a better shaper of the children's character, present and future. She becomes more serviceable to her Master.

Cleansing is also more important than most people think. It includes both inner and outer cleansing. Some people who bathe fastidiously would be shocked at their filthy inner condition inside.

Health, it is sometimes said, depends on three things: food, assimilation, and elimination. That is, enough of the right sort of food, the ability to digest and absorb it into the body, *and* the prompt elimination of all the waste.

It is surprising how much waste there is to be thrown out. Nature provides two ways for its removal, through the skin and through certain inner organs. A healthy body takes care of its own waste products.

Careful, prayerful obedience to the laws of the body builds a healthy body. Careless indifference is apt to dirty the *inside* of the body. Bathing, and especially preserving the bodily rhythm, receive the attention of the thoughtful Christian.

Posture is also important for good health. Man is the one upright animal of all creation, but Americans seem to forget this fact. Our habit of slumping down in the chair, sitting on the small of the back, and drooping at the shoulders is a serious problem. The vital organs get crowded for space. The whole inner machine is badly disturbed. The habit of upright posture, standing and sitting and walking, affects one's health enormously. But proper posture is impossible without easy-fitting low-heeled shoes.

The Blood Is the Life

The Bible says: "the blood is the life." In fact, the scriptures contain many passages about blood. The deep spiritual significance in many of them is the reference to the sacrifice of Christ. But apart from that teaching, it also includes a great truth for our bodily health. The blood is indeed the life of our bodies.

The bone marrow makes blood, the heart pumps it, the lungs oxygenate it, and remove carbon dioxide, proper exercise keeps it in proper circulation. The whole bodily rhythm is concerned with the blood, its quality and quantity and its proper circulation. Good blood, in right quantity, kept moving naturally through the body, results in full vigorous life. Poor blood, not enough blood, means a poor, defective quality of life. Congested blood, too much in one part and too little somewhere else, means disorder, disease.

Enough blood, not too much of the right quality, not too rich, in normal circulation, gives vigorous and abundant physical life. Any slip at any point means either defective or diseased life. And the sort of food decides the sort of blood.

These are the six things suggested by those two old models of personal life: food, air, exercise, sleep, cleansing, and posture. They come under the head of obedience, the second of the two main points we are discussing.

Bodily Sins

Some of the most common sins are not considered sins at all. Yet they *are* sins against our bodies, *and* thus against him who dwells within us.

Here are the most common sins against the body: too much food and an unbalanced diet; lack of balanced exercise; taking poisons into the body in the shape of stimulants, sedatives, and drugs; tense nerves; overwork; and the use of the propagating organs otherwise than as intended by nature.

Bodily sin is responsible for the greatest number of diseases. Repentance here would result in most physicians losing their practice. But there seems little need for the physicians to worry on this score.

Of course, overwork is one of the most common sins among conscientious Christians. It may come through a lack of judgment. Most times it is, at root, evidence of a lack of practical faith in Christ.

There are no breakdowns in the path of obedience. But the path of service is strewn thick with saintly wrecks. The touchstone of the true life is, not the crowds and their need, not service, not suffering nor sacrifice.

The touchstone is obedience; simple, clear, intelligent, full obedience to the Holy Spirit's leading. When we are in doubt, we should wait.

There's a Lord to our harvest. There's a Chief of Staff. The ordering of strategy and tactics and movements belongs to him. Our part is the quiet heart, the open ear, the trained discernment of his voice, and his leading. Our part is to do as he leads, *and to do only that.*

The thing to remember constantly is this: it is Christ's will to forgive the truly penitent and to heal their bodies. He is at your side now eagerly waiting to do whatever is needed.

SEVEN

God's School of Suffering

It is Christ's first will that we should be made pure in heart, intelligent in understanding the Father's will, with a passion for doing it, out of touch with everything that doesn't help, in warm touch with our fellowmen, inflexibly set against every sort of evil, and always strong and healthful in body.

Guard Your Strong Points

Experience is the best teacher and charges the biggest fee. It insists on being paid, day by day, as you go along. You don't pay simply with gold and engraved paper and checks. No, you pay with blood and sweat. You pay with your own life given slowly, sometimes painfully, under tense pressure.

But you receive the one real thing, the real gold of character; your changed self, that's what you get. You are never the same again.

Experience is both what you go through, and what goes through you. True knowledge is limited to just that. We know only what we experience. What is woven into the fabric of actual life, that we really know, and only that. The rest we only know *about*. There is a great difference between the two.

Bodily pain bends the most stubborn will, and that is saying a great deal. For there is nothing harder to bend than a stubborn will. The will is never broken. It can't be. It can only be bent, and that means bent from within. No one's will, however obstinate, can be bent, however slightly, except from within. That is to say, by one's own choosing to bend it.

Every person is an absolute sovereign in will, from our mother's breast until the breast of old mother-earth enfolds us at the last. This is the way God made us.

But bodily pain, cutting, eating in, and then getting sharper-toothed, and persisting, tirelessly persisting, day in and day out, by night and day, awake and asleep, that is the sorest pressure that can be brought to bear on the will. It is the whip with the ugliest lash and sting.

Often, it is stubborn self-will and love in fierce competition. The self-will refuses to bend even when it knows it should. For stubbornness can become a habit gripping a person beyond one's own wish. And love, with a breaking heart over the pain being suffered by that stubborn will, yet keeps the fire burning more fiercely, *to save the person's life*.

One can be strong enough to be stubborn, but not strong enough to bend. The will is really strongest when it uses its strength in bending to a higher, better, wiser, will.

But Love wins out. The exceptions are rare. The heart, after all, wins in competition with the will. It kindles gentle, fierce fires under the will, and keeps them burning, tender and hot, till the will yields, mellows, bends, capitulates.

The one thing greater than a stubborn will is a true, tender, hot heart. Love wins. This is the great lesson in God's school of suffering.

A person's strong point is apt to become a weak point, when that person is out of full touch with God. Away from the steadying touch of God's presence the pendulum swings clear to the opposite limit. Abraham was called a friend of God because he believed him. His faith in God did not stagger at the humanly impossible. Yet Abraham failed God, twice, in going to Egypt and so imperiling God's world plan; and in the Hagar incident.

Moses was a meek man, but no one ever lost his temper so completely. David was one of the saintliest of men, and yet he had an ugly moral blot in his life. Solomon was once the wisest man.

But later he became the stupidest moral fool and so continued to the end. Elijah's boldness and daring was unparalleled, yet he ran away with cowardly swiftness from a woman's threat.

Job was esteemed the most patient of men, but was there ever a greater exhibition of hot, intolerant impatience than in his replies to his critics? He was the humblest of saints, and unconsciously showed how proud a man could be.

One should keep a keen eye on his strong points. "Eyesight" is keenest when the knees are bent.

Man is free, utterly free, *in* his will. That's God's tenderest touch. In freedom of will is where man is most like God. One may become a slave, a rank slave, shackled and chained *to* his will because of the ugly trail of sin, the getting out of touch with God.

It's Christ's *first* will that we should be strong and well in body. But our wills often get in the way of Christ's. Some of the saintliest of people, so lovable and gentle personally, have stubborn wills. Let us hope that they do so *unconsciously*. So there has to be a term of school. Saints take the part of the scholars and provide the entrance conditions for the school of suffering. The discipline seems stiff and stern and the fees very high. They are payable daily, but the lessons seem hard.

Love is always the schoolmaster, real Love, tender and true, honest and courageous, uncompromisingly insistent on the highest ideals.

One hand tenderly and patiently is underneath strengthening and sustaining, while the other guides and steadies, limits and lessens, the discipline when possible. The Schoolmaster's eye watches the calendar hoping for an early graduation. His heart watches with deep concern the scholar, who alone fixes the graduation date.

We learn best by stories and pictures. The story is the picture for the ear. The picture is the story for the eye. We learn most through the eye, with the ear a close second.

There are three stories in the Bible pictured stories with the warm, vivid coloring of real human life. Job is at one end, Paul at the other, and Jacob in between. Any one of them is adequate for telling the story of love's schooling, all three together build up to the irresistible point.

Job the Scholar

Fascination surrounds the story of Job because it is told so fully, and made so vivid, and is so human. It deals with the sorest question of human life through the ages, the problem of suffering. Here, simply told, put into men's hands at once, is God's own answer to the problem. And it proves an answer that answers. It is full and adequate.

It is striking that there are two parts to Job's story. The first has caught the eye of the church; the second part has been strangely slighted, indeed ignored. Yet the story is not complete, and the answer not understood, unless and until both parts are taken together. It is one story.

There are six sections in the story, all told. Part one includes five sections, and part two is made up of just one section.

But what a section this sixth is. It vibrates with joy. Music and exuberant singing fill the air. Laughter and congratulation, praise to God, and happy fellowship among men echo everywhere. The sun is shining. The birds burst their throats with song. The very air is alive with human gladness. And the music is now in the major key. The minor chording that swept and wept all through part one becomes a blessed undertone in part two to make the joy of the major stand out in bolder relief.

Look, briefly, at the six sections of Job. Section one is *the scholar in school*. The picture is drawn from others' views of him. It describes his common reputation in the whole countryside. He was holy and upright in all his dealings with his fellows. He also revered God and earnestly sought to please him.

Whenever his family took a time of feasting and convivial enjoyment, Job was careful to have a special time of prayer afterward, asking that if anything had been done or said that displeased God it might be forgiven. It was his conscientious habit to be pleasing to God in the whole fabric of his life. And he was careful to guard the life of his growing family.

Job's very name suggests his character. Names grew up in those days, out of a man's character. Here the name given has spiritual significance. That would be natural with such a man, for his saintliness, his holiness was the outstanding trait. He was called *Job,* that is, the man hated, hounded, persecuted to the utmost possible limit.

His character made him hated. He was heartily disliked by those of opposite character. Especially he was hated by the unseen spirit Prince of Evil, whose existence and personality in that early day was never questioned.

This is the picture other people saw, a man so conscientious, so upright, so thoughtfully and methodically righteous and saintly as to arouse opposition in some quarters.

There's another description of Job that comes out later in the story. It was the side that God saw the *in*side of his character. He was so humble that, probably unconsciously, he was proud of his humility. He held a subtle, unsuspected inner satisfaction with his spiritual attainments.

What a strange bit of irony, pride in being humble! But a snake may crawl noiselessly through the greenest grass and among the most fragrant flowers.

He was so conscientious in planning his life to make it pleasing to God that he slipped a bit in living it. Without being aware of it, that conscientiousness, methodical care, and saintliness of habit got into his inner subconsciousness even more than God himself.

Job would have been the first to change had he recognized the tendency. He was quick to repent when God actually spoke to him, and things got straightened out.

That's the man, the scholar in the school, the two men in one—the man his neighbors saw, and the man God saw. That's section one (Jb 1:1-5). Men saw a humble, godly man. God saw a bit of dross in the rare fine gold of this man's character.

Job's First Session of School

Section two is the *first session of school*. In the spiritual realm above there's a reviewing of things down on the earth. Satan is spoken of for the first time in the scriptures, and spoken of by that name, the Satan, the accuser, the hater, the hounder of men.

God takes the initiative regarding Job. This is

significant because it shows God had a purpose. God speaks of the well-known character of Job. Satan maliciously slanders Job as an utterly selfish man who finds it to his advantage to be righteous. Satan is given permission to interfere in Job's affairs, but within strict limits (Jb 1:6-12).

Then the scene of the story shifts to the earth again. Job's opportunity has come. The door upstairs is to open at his feet.

War, marauding bands, lightning, a terrific windstorm come one after the other with a rush. Everything is swept away in quick succession, including children.

Calamities pile up as the story is told to Job, by one breathless messenger after another.

In this hour of bereavement, with torn and bleeding heart, Job never flinched in his simple trust in God and his unfailing personal devotion to him. Things have gone awfully bad. But there is no reproach in Job's heart.

It is significant that the immediate origin of his trouble is unrecognized. He supposes that it is God himself causing disaster after disaster (Jb 1:21). It gives emphasis to his humble, uncomplaining submission to God, though he can't understand *why* such things should happen to him.

Again the scene shifts to the upper realm, and again God speaks of the righteousness of Job, though so severely tried. Again Satan slanders and imputes selfish motives. And now God withdraws the restriction on Job's person, within a strict limit (Jb 2:1-6).

Then comes the touch on Job's person. One of the worst plagues known in that subtropical climate is known as the black leprosy of Egypt. This breaks out in Job's body. God's gracious protecting restraint is partially withdrawn, for a brief time (Jb 2:7-13).

Poor saintly Job, sitting on an ash heap, scraping his itching sores with the sharp edge of a broken piece of crockery. The scene takes hold of one's heart.

Next his wife loses heart, and incoherently, bitterly cries out against God. It's a bitter draft to swallow when a man doesn't feel his wife by his side, close up, steadying and believing in him.

Soon the three neighbors come. They are supposed to be comforters, deeply grieved over their old neighbor's plight. For seven silent days and seven yet more silent nights they sit looking. Peering aslant and direct, at Job and at each other, with never a word spoken, but many a thought, they sit.

That was the decisive stroke. Job broke under the stress. His keen ear heard their unspoken thoughts. His sensitive spirit felt the cutting edge of those peering eyes. Loss of property, loss of children, loss of health, loss of his wife's sympathetic fellowship, he stood up under these. But loss of his sacred privacy, and then the criticism all the keener and more cutting because unspoken, and unbroken seven days and seven sleepless nights, were too much. Little wonder!

The time test is the hardest test. The patience of patient Job ran out. With cunning, Satan planned that campaign, devilishly, cruelly, heartlessly cunning. This is section two, the first session in school.

Job: Inside

Then comes section three, *the unsuspected man inside is revealed* (Jb 3:1-31:40). "After this," this sevenfold cunningly piled-up climax of attack, Job "cursed his day."

That is, tacitly, probably unintentionally, he cursed God who gave the creative touch that day of his birth.

For bitterness of spirit, biting sarcasm, persistent absorption in his own integrity and in the unfairness of all that was happening to him, for rebellion against God and God's dealings, it would be difficult to match Job in the flood of talk that now comes. How pain itself, with no touch of grace allowed in, sharpens the tongue, makes picturesque rhetoric, and puts acid in the spittle! It is immensely suggestive.

The three critics, called comforters, go at him

in turn. And the burden of their talk is this: all these calamities mean that God is acting in judgment on Job for his wickedness. They insist that all his godliness is a mere sham to cover up the utter selfishness and actual wickedness underneath. Their talk hangs together well, and is full of pious phraseology, inaccuracies, half truths, and positive untruths. It's a queer tangle and mixture. It has a strangely familiar modern sound.

It is not difficult to understand who sent them, or which side they represent in this pathetic conflict. It's the last stroke of that carefully planned attack. One should be careful with quotations from the Book of Job, to note whose words are being quoted.

But Job out-talks the three critics. As the debate goes on, their talks get shorter, his longer. He talks nine times, all three of them eight times. His bitterness increases, and at last they quit. They are talked out. The case is hopeless to them because this man Job is so set on believing in his own righteousness. They give Job up as a hopeless incorrigible.

This is the first session of the school, and Job blunders badly on the exam. Job lays himself bare. He is indeed a rare saint in the utter integrity of his heart and life. But Job questioned God's love, which is always above question or suspicion.

Because he doesn't understand, he questions God's love; he doubts it.

In that sore experience, unsuspected weaknesses that were inside came out. As you see them coming out you know that they were hidden away inside.

Sitting on the ash heap, talking, with the sharp-edged bit of broken crockery in rhythmic motion on his itching scabs, Job declares his own righteousness, and reviling God and God's dealings. Cutting, sarcastic flings intermingle with insistence on his faith in God.

The examinations go hard for Job. They show up something inside never suspected. He doesn't see it yet. His humility is the last thing in view now.

Where *is* the proverbial patience of patient Job? All this rebelliousness of spirit against God, this biting, burning sarcasm, this utter absence of the love spirit, this utter depressed absorption in himself, this exaggerated ego, this had all been on the inside, unsuspected.

One begins to understand now about that school of suffering. The graduate, with honors, of many schools is having a final post-graduate course. God wants to raise him up higher, highest, with full honors, but forgetting all about the honors in giving full attention to his wondrous God.

In section four, *God's teacher comes* (Jb 32:1-37:24). The second session of school opens. God takes a hand in things indirectly. He sends a messenger, Elihu. Elihu is a *teacher*. What poor, saintly, righteous Job needed above all things just now was a teacher.

His heart was all right, but his understanding was muddled. The teacher quietly, patiently, gently, plainly, teaches. Then Job's eyes begin to open. New soft light begins to break in.

First, this teacher explains just *why* all this has happened to Job. He repudiates what the three critics had been declaring so positively. God had *not* been acting in judgment on Job. The whole thing is on a wholly higher level, a love level.

Elihu points out that Job had been insisting on his own integrity. He was rebelling bitterly because of what had happened to him, and against God's dealings with him, and so against God himself (Jb 33:8-12).

Job had been proud of his sanctity, the utter uprightness of his conduct, and the sincerity of his heart. He had become absorbed with himself, his saintliness. He was unconsciously proud of being humble (Jb 33:17).

Pride is being taken up with yourself in any degree or any way, and not letting God in, in his own place. Humility is letting God into one's thought and imagination and purpose, *as big as he really is.* All we have is from God, a direct gift to be held in trust.

Talents, gifts, powers, possessions, everything is given by him. It is a trust in the full legal meaning of that word, and in the higher love meaning. All these gifts are at their best only as God's touch is upon them in full.

No one is true to himself, and to his powers, and to his neighbors, except as all are yielded up to God's touch, his full constant touch. When that's so, the mind, the imagination, the will, are all absorbed with the thought of God himself, his love so beyond words, and all that grows out of his love.

Pride is the assertion of one's self. Humility is being so taken up with some One else that one thinks of himself only in relation to that One. In a simple, practical, wholesome way all one's powers, one's relation to his fellows and to the day's task, fall into the right place. That comes from the touch of this One you are so taken up with.

Absorption in God, in Christ, is a practical thing. You have seen a babe watching intently the mother's face, utterly absorbed, conscious of nothing else. And the sight caught your heart.

Humility is the mother with her babe, a lover with his loved one, a husband with a wife. This thing of being absorbed in someone else is common enough to know about, blessedly so.

Job was being wooed from absorption in himself up to a higher level, forgetting himself in seeing God. If ever a man really sees God, he loses himself at once. Yet he really gets hold of his true self in losing himself in God.

Elihu gently but firmly puts his finger on the sore spot. Job had been taken up with himself. His whole trouble was pride, thinking about himself (Jb 33:13-18). That's the teacher's first point, tactfully and clearly made.

Elihu continues, and speaks about Job's sickness. He touches upon only one thing in Job's troubles, but that is enough to clear Job's understanding.

Elihu doesn't talk about the process by which the disease came to Job. Instead, he gives a vivid description of a desperately sick man (Jb 33:19-22).

A teacher comes to speak to this sick man (Jb 33:23). Elihu refers to himself only indirectly. Here a paraphrase helps make the thought clearer.

Elihu says, "If there be with the sick man a messenger, a teacher, one in the close, confidential touch of personal love, to explain things to him patiently and gently and clearly . . ."

Then comes prayer and the healing (Jb 33:24-28). The healed man frankly confesses his sin and goes about singing. He is so absorbed with the wondrous God he has found, that he goes about telling his neighbors and friends about him.

This is the heart of Elihu's teaching. There are six links in its chain: pride, disease, a teacher, prayer, healing, telling others about this wondrous God.

The rest of Elihu's talk, by far the greater part, is taken up chiefly in *talking about God.* Unconsciously, he becomes a fine illustration of what he is talking about.

I can imagine that a restful sigh escaped Job's lips. His thought is sharply changed. What fine psychology! He turns away from himself (what a relief!) to *God* (Jb 34-37). That's the close of the second session of school.

Job Sees God

The third session opens in the fifth chapter of the story, and *Job gets a sight of God* (Jb 38-41). God speaks. Job hears, and gets down on his face at once. God picks up the thread where Elihu had dropped it and goes on weaving the same fabric. What God does is simply this: he looks into Job's face. Job never forgot the sight. God talks in a very simple way about himself.

Job gets a picture of God, the Creator, his intelligence that could think things out, his wisdom that could so skillfully adapt means to end, his power that could actually do what he did;

and then above all, running through all and between the lines is his love.

Job got a picture of God. He never got over it. He fell down on his face in the dust. It's a remarkable turnaround. "Mine eye seeth *Thee*: I abhor *myself*" (Jb 42:1-9). Then God graciously gives Job a rare opportunity. It is not a test to see if Job can stand it. It is Job's opportunity to reveal the wholly new spirit now in control. It is his opportunity to be like God.

He is to pray for these poor, befogged critics. They certainly need it. And he gladly does it. He is so taken up now with God that everything is affected. The absorbing thought of such a God comes flooding in. It takes possession. It graciously grips him.

The bitter sarcasm toward these critics wastes away. Love, that is to say, God, fills his heart. He is grateful for the outlet of this new passion. He gladly prays for these men that they, too, may see this wondrous God.

The real God-touch means a more human touch. Job has true humility now, but he doesn't know it. He's so absorbed with God that he quickly forgives and loves his bitter critics. That's being like God. That's the God-touch.

When a man thinks he is humble, he may know at once that he isn't. He is thinking about himself. When one thinks in his heart that he really *is* saintly, he may know for certain that he isn't. He hasn't the real thing, for he's taken up with himself.

Real humility means being absorbed with God—becoming unconsciously like him. It becomes a passion, an intensely practical passion, to get others in touch too. That's the God-touch.

Humility is such a sensitive plant. When you think you have it, it withers up at once, and dies. This is the third session of school. Job sees God, and gets down on his face, and then reaches out to help others.

Then comes section six, *Graduation Day* (Jb 42:10-17). School's out. Satan is heard of no more. He has slunk away. Resisted, he fled. The healing touch comes without being asked for. And it's a full healing. It includes body and family and circumstances and length of life.

The striking thing is this: *Job fixed the date for graduation day.* The whole decision rested with him. His will had new strength now. It could bend, bend to the higher will. And it did. That was the turning point. That fixed the date. All God's power and love await man's consent. We control the door through which God enters our lives.

How long did this school of suffering last? There were three sessions, then graduation day. But how much time did the whole take? I don't know in actual days and weeks. It doesn't tell. But the story as told gives the impression that the whole thing could have occurred within a few weeks, from new moon to full.

How long did this school last? I do know. I know exactly. Just as long as it took Job to get down on his face; then came graduation day.

Job could have made it last much longer. Anyone can. Some are strong enough to talk humbly about themselves, and submissively. But they are not strong enough to bend, bend clear down.

You have to bend all the way down to see God's face and hear his voice. The best view of God is gotten when on your face in the dust. Then the eyes of the spirit open. Even the ash heap and that broken piece of crockery become fragrant memories. For they were the gateway into that blessed change of spirit.

School fees were never so high. Ask Job. And payment of fees was never more cheerfully assented to, *afterward,* when school was out.

One is quick to note that there is a twofold purpose in this old Job school-story. There was a purpose *for* Job himself. *And* there was a purpose *through* Job. Job has been a silent, eloquent preacher to men ever since his story was lived in the plains and hills of Uz. There was a distinct purpose of service in Job's experience. The whole church, and someday the whole race, will be grateful to Job for being a good scholar in God's school.

Paul's Thorn: The Man

The second of these outstanding picture stories is that of Paul, Paul's thorn. Whenever one talks positively about prayer, or about bodily healing, someone always remembers and asks about Paul's thorn.

First a look at the man, then a look at his thorn. The best light on this troublesome thorn is the man. Paul himself, his character, and the great work for God he was chosen to do, these throw the best light on that stinging, sticking thorn.

Paul is a great man from any point of view, and a great saint. His Hebrew blood, his aristocratic family and breeding, his inherited and acquired culture, his university training, his breadth of outlook, his inflexible conscientiousness, his passion of devotion to his Master—what a man among men he was! What a saint among saints! What a giant he was in his will! The unflinching unfaltering insistence on his task, in spite of opposition and difficulties, including all those arduous journeys in the thick of hardships up to the limit of endurance—these all tell what a giant he was in his will.

But, speak softly, his strong will sometimes held the lines too tightly. A man's weak point is apt to be the swing-away of the pendulum on his strong point. Paul had the weakness of his strongest qualities. He was set in his way.

Say it very softly, for we are talking about Saint Paul. Say it yet more softly, for where one speaks of one weak spot in him, he quickly calls to mind a half-dozen in himself. Yet say it distinctly, *to help*.

God had a hard time getting Paul to go *his* way. God found it difficult sometimes to get Paul to fit into *his* plans. Paul had a plan or two of his own. This may sound familiar to one or two of us.

From the time of that never-to-be-forgotten experience on the Damascus road, with the light, and the voice, and the overwhelming sense of power, Paul knew that his errand was to the outer non-Jewish world.

The nations of the earth, the gentiles, these made up his field of service. The very magnitude of it must have appealed to the imagination of this saint.

But, from the first, he had an intense desire to go to the Jerusalem Jews. It was perfectly natural, for Paul had been so closely associated with them. And his very sense of strategy in action suggested and emphasized it. He felt it in his bones, "I know them. I trained with that group, and I know how to take them. Let me at them. If once we can get *them,* it will mean so much.

"It's the strategic thing. They crucified Jesus. They stoned the Holy Spirit, in effect, in stoning Stephen. But, *but,* let me at them." This was deep down in his spirit.

Early in his Christian life, Paul received a special vision about this very matter when he was praying in the sacred precincts of the temple in Jerusalem (Acts 22:17-21). The Lord gave him specific directions to get out of Jerusalem, out to the non-Jewish world. The Jerusalem leaders were incorrigibly set in their stubborn rejection, he was told.

Then a strange thing happened. Paul actually began to argue with the Lord and explain why he was specially qualified for a Jewish mission! This was surely taking things to great length—the soldier under orders arguing with the Chief of Staff why he should not do as he was bid. Did Paul's intensity blur his thinking?

The temple interview closes with a clear command: "Depart; for I will send thee *far hence* [from Jerusalem] to the outer non-Jewish peoples."

And Paul went. With all his splendid powers and devotion, he went. But he never lost that passionate inner longing. He insisted upon it, years after, against distinct intimations of the

Holy Spirit in line with that temple vision (Acts 21:4).

That's a little glimpse at this rare, saintly giant of God. It explains the thorn that came, and was not taken away.

Paul's Thorn: Healing While Not Healed

Now, about the thorn (2 Cor 12:7-10). Paul contracted some serious ailment in his body. No one knows what it was. The long, learned discussions are wasted breath, when time is so precious and real things so pressing. It doesn't matter what it was. It was there, and it stayed. It interfered. It hurt keenly.

Paul didn't think so much of it at first. He had Christ to go to. He would go and ask for healing. And the healing touch would come, he felt sure.

All Paul's experience would lead him to expect the healing touch. He had that remarkable two years' campaign in Ephesus, where healings to a quite unusual degree were the outstanding healings (Acts 19:10-12).

Earlier there had been the man crippled from birth, never able to walk, now leaping and walking through Christ's touch, at the word of Paul (Acts 14:8-10).

In a yet more remarkable passage, a young man at Troas on the Aegean, actually brought back from the dead by Paul. And Paul had taught healing. It was part of his group of teachings to the churches wherever he went. He himself had known the healing touch. He had the best of reasons for expecting healing now. Indeed he seems not to have doubted that the healing touch would come. But it didn't.

He prayed specifically for healing, but still there was no change. The thorn stayed. Its needle point gets sharper, and sticks persistently in. A third time Paul goes to his knees. How earnestly some of us can understand.

Now, notice, that Paul's prayer is answered. The answer contains three items. First of all, the man is answered though the petition is denied. Paul is not ignored. His prayer is heard. Christ never ignores anyone, nor fails to hear any honest prayer.

The second thing to note is just what Christ said in his answer. I can see Paul one night all alone with his thorn. The day's work is done, the stitching of tent canvas, the talking to the crowds and to the two's and three's.

He is tired. He has gone to bed. He would sleep but for that thorn. He turns and twists, and longs for the sleep that doesn't come. He wonders why the healing touch hasn't come. He is a little perplexed and maybe depressed.

Then, very quietly, a voice comes, an inner voice, quiet as Hermon's dew, clear as the tone of a bell. The voice says, "Paul, I know about that thorn, and how it hurts. It hurts me, too. It hurts me because it hurts you.

"But, Paul," the voice goes quietly, steadily on, "it's a bit better to let the thorn stay, because, only so can I have the use of you, the full free use of you, in *my* plans for the world I gave my life's blood for."

A hush comes over the dear man's spirit. There comes with the voice a look within. Instinctively, Paul begins to understand better. A soft, clear light breaks. He knows, at once, the truth of the word being gently spoken. He knows that the diagnosis is accurate. And he lies quiet, with a great deep hush in his inner spirit. That's the second part of the answer.

The voice comes again. When the pause has deepened the impression, more comes. The voice goes on in yet quieter, gentler lingering tones, "Paul, I'll be so near you, you will have such a sense of my presence, that you'll forget the thorn even while you feel it cutting in."

Years after, I can see Paul in his own hired house in Rome. It's late at night. The crowds have been thronging the house, crowds from all over the world. An Egyptian sits over there, and a dark-skinned Ethiopian here.

A cultured-faced man from the Euphrates and a fair-skinned Caucasian stand in the corner, side by side. Keen-eyed Greeks, vigorous Latins, alert, courtly Spaniards, the cultured and the scholarly, the unlettered and the folks, gently jostle each other.

They crowd in, listening intently, and questioning eagerly. The unseen Presence is excitingly real. And Paul's heart is all aglow. They slip out into the night. Once again the burning Christ message has gone out to the whole world.

Paul is sitting quietly, slowing down inside before seeking bed and sleep. One arm is around young Timothy, not so young now. The other hand is laid caressingly upon dear faithful Doctor Luke's arm.

They're talking in subdued tones. And as you listen in, you hear Paul say, "Do you know, dear old friends, I wouldn't have missed the thorn for the presence . . ."

And the sentence breaks off. A bit of hoarseness, the hoarseness of deep emotion, thickens his voice. And the look of deep reverence mingled with love deepens in his companions' faces.

Then he goes quietly on, ". . . the presence, the wondrous glory-presence of Jesus, beyond words, that has been with me through it all."

And the clearer light breaks on his listeners. The inner understanding deepens. A great silence falls on them. They know they are at the deep springs.

They are being allowed to see the Lord's love for his world, and the place this grayed veteran is having in it. The emergency of sin has gripped both—the unseen One and this man so great in his suffering and in his service.

Yet there's something more to add. I am clear, and I grow yet clearer, that our Lord Jesus still prefers to take the thorn away. And he will *if* he may have his way, his *first* way.

Graduation day comes later to Paul. It came one day just outside that city, with an escort of imperial Roman soldiers. Yet (very softly and still very distinctly, let the words be spoken) it might have come sooner.

It is significant to note here that Paul was repeatedly conscious, indeed continuously conscious of Christ's healing touch on his body. As one reads the whole story through, it becomes obvious that Christ's healing touch, in protection, in strengthening, and in actual healing, was with Paul through all those thorn years.

It is difficult, if not impossible, to fit in chronologically the beginning of this distressing ailment. But remember that Paul had been left for dead just outside Lystra in Asia Minor. And the intense hatred of the Antioch Jews would make them do a thorough job of stoning. Their efficiency is beyond question. Yet Paul gets up, rests over night, and pushes on the next day. He apparently carried out the itinerary as planned. That would be an outstanding instance of healing under most extreme circumstances.

No one can read Paul's own long remarkable

list of the experiences he went through without a lasting impression of Christ's direct touch on his body throughout.

Listen, and think about it. Five times he had been whipped on his bare back with forty-stripes-save-one. And three times with the yet more severe Roman rods. He was once stoned, three times shipwrecked, and was a night and a day drifting exposed out in the open sea.

He was exposed to the acute hardship of the crude traveling of that time, perils of swollen rivers, of robbers not hesitating to use violence, of hunger and thirst, of cold and insufficient clothing.

Think slowly about that list. Clearly enough, the experience with the thorn was the more striking to Paul because it happened in the midst of Christ's constant healing touch upon Paul's body. Paul experienced the threefold healing: the continual protecting restraint upon disease, the strengthening of bodily functions, and the direct positive healing. Or else he could never have gone through what he did. The thorn was the more marked as an exception in the midst of such experience.

The thing that stands out biggest in the whole story is this: it was for the sake of service that this thorn was allowed. It was for the sake of a race of human beings drowning in sin, that the thing occurred.

It was exceptional. Had it been merely Paul involved the whole trend of Christ's dealing makes clear that this ailment would have gone like the others. But service controlled. The world's emergency took precedence.

Jacob's Limp

One more picture in this rare old gallery of honest portraits is the picture of Jacob at Jabbok (Gn 32:24-32).

In that struggle at night between the sturdy Hebrew herdsman and an unrecognized assailant, Jacob fully holds his own. Then toward dawn the assailant does a strange thing.

Jacob is startled to feel a slight touch on the inner side of his thigh, and at once the thigh bone goes out of joint. Instantly, Jacob knows that this is no mere man. No man could have done that. And two things at least crowd his mind faster than he can think.

He knows that he has lost his ability to wrestle. But, far deeper, comes the recognition of who this unrecognized stranger is.

He's been fighting against God! And all these years he had been fighting against God, and against God's plans for his life! Unconsciously fighting? Half consciously fighting?

It's the one instance in scripture of God's own direct touch on a man's body, injuring, laming him. Notice that it was not a disease. It was a slowing down of the man's gait. He had been so sure of himself. Now he must go through life halting, limping.

God had a purpose for this exceptional act. He always has a purpose, and it is always a purpose of love. Jacob was hindering, actually holding back, and threatening to block completely, God's world plan. It wasn't merely Jacob's own life that was concerned. God's plan for the race hinged on this man.

A man may hinder or break God's plan for his own life, if he will. All God's plans wait on our consent. The sovereign God waits on the sovereignty of man's choice. But no man can break God's broad plan for the world. He may slow it up. He does that often. God's sovereignty simply means that, ultimately, through the intricate network of human wills, his great plan will work out, and always in some way *through* man's choice, freely given.

Even now, Jacob could have balked still further. It wasn't merely the touch of *power* on his thigh that won. It was that, plus something more, far deeper and more tender. It was the touch of *love* upon his heart.

Jacob could have fought against the power. But the love, the patient waiting and putting up with his wayward conduct all these long years, the gracious wooing, in so many ways!—he could see it all now. It was this that bent his will at last, from serving himself, to obeying this strong, waiting, loving will of his great God. Note that this is *a crisis*. Most reverently it can be said it was *God's* crisis. God's plan was in danger. The world's salvation was at issue.

It is a threefold crisis. It was *a crisis of available material*. Jacob was the son of Isaac, the grandson of Abraham, through whom the world plan must be worked out. He was the twin son, it is true. But the other, Esau, was plainly disqualified by temperament. Impulsive, hot-headed, wholly unreliable, bartering his most sacred possession for something to eat, as unstable as water, he was wholly unfit for leadership in carrying forward God's plan. God was narrowed down to Jacob.

Jacob was a cool, steady, calculating man of method and habit. He was a thinker and a hard worker. He was a man to do things. But he had the mean moral strain in him. He was intensely selfish. He was forever grasping, cunningly taking advantage of other people. He was unscrupulous. He never hesitated at the most underhanded move to gain his position. Jacob was morally contemptible. But his failings were moral. Esau's were mental. The moral could be changed by grace, if Jacob's consent could be gotten.

It was not really that Jacob was the better man, he was the less-poor of the two. It was a crisis of available material. God needs the best. He needed

Jacob, but first Jacob had to change. So the exceptional was done.

It was *a crisis of time*. For long years God patiently waited for Abraham and Sarah to change their hearts. Isaac was the child of the changed Abraham and Sarah. He took on their later traits.

And now, for many long years, a full quarter of a century at least, God had been calling Jacob up to the higher level. But Jacob's firmness and strength teetered over into stubbornness.

He grew more stubborn, more obstinate, more set than ever. Time pressed. The stubbornness grew more, and then yet more. In a crisis of time God did the exceptional thing.

It was *a world crisis*. God's plan concerned a world. A Babel, a Flood, a Sodom-and-Gomorrah, tremendous moral catastrophes, these told plainly the moral outcome threatening.

Through Jacob and Jacob's line was to come the little messenger-nation, the Savior-nation, the Savior himself. All unknown, unsuspected by any but God, it was the world crisis. For the sake of the race, to save his great plan for saving a world, God did the exceptional thing.

So, by the fords of the Jabbok, under that gentle touch of supernatural power, at the break of a new day, Jacob surrendered his proud stubborn will.

The touch on Jacob's thigh was meant for his

heart, like the later touch on the disciples' feet. Jacob felt it there, and his heart broke. He had actually been fighting God! He never really meant to do that.

That heart-breaking touch on the thigh reached into the will, the citadel. The will bent. With all its disciplined strength it bent, and bent all the way over. He quit wrestling. He had to. The disabled thigh settled the wrestling. He took to clinging. And he became the prince, the Israel, pleading for forgiveness and blessing, and prevailing.

God yielded to that penitent, clinging plea. God had saved two, the man and the world-plan. The world-plan was saved through the man. No one ever knows how much hangs on saying yes to God.

Jacob learned to walk with God, by *limping*. God tried to get him to walk without the limp. He preferred that. He still does. Jacob got along faster now because he had been slowed down. He never walked so fast in his life in the true path as when he went slowly, limping along in his body.

One can well understand that God did what he did reluctantly. It was an emergency transaction. All the world is in an emergency *just now*. And God is still needing men.

These are the three pictures in this old gallery: Job's ulcerous boils and the ash heap schoolhouse, Paul's needle-pointed thorn, and Jacob's halting limp.

These are three scholars in God's school of suffering. Job graduated early. He learned quickly. It was an intense session but a short one, intensive school work. Paul's graduation came later, as did Jacob's. Have they had a reunion up there, these three, in the Teacher's own presence, praising him together with full hearts? I think it likely.

Note that in each case the man concerned was a leader. That makes a great difference. The Devil lays special siege to the leaders. Leaders need more schooling because they touch the lives of so many.

Yet no one lives to himself. None of us can tell what plan of service to Christ may center in our glad consent to his personal plan for our life. In each case it was a crisis, the meeting place of dismal failure and glorious victory. And the man was always the decisive factor.

One recognizes crises best looking *backwards*. We are so much wiser, *afterwards*. If only we might be quick and true to obey, for Christ's sake, *before* we know it may be a crisis for someone or some plan.

Keep Your Hand Out

So there may be a waiting time. Bodily healing may be needed, desperately needed perhaps. And we may be in real touch of heart with Christ. We may pray for the healing touch. Yet, it may not come. There may be a waiting time.

If so, it means simply that we need some schooling. There's some plan involved. What is required is to be good scholars. We should cultivate the keen inner ear and the quiet inner spirit, so we can hear the Teacher's voice. For he is speaking, and if we are still enough we will hear.

No one expects to stay in school all through life. We should look forward to a glad graduation day. We should plan early graduation. Our hands should be stretched out, stretched expectantly out, till they grasp what has been promised.

I can never forget my mother's very brief paraphrase of that long verse from the Book of Malachi (Mal 3:10). The verse begins, you remember, "bring ye the whole tithe *in,*" and it ends up with "I will pour" the blessing *out.*

My mother's brief paraphrase was this: *Give all he asks; take all he promises.*

Within recent years, I went through a critical illness, happily not prolonged. God made it clear to me that there was a purpose behind my illness. I am still in school, God's school. I have gotten through some of the rooms, but not all. My hand is stretched out day and night. And I have the sweet assurance that graduation day is coming very soon now.

I heard a simple story of a New York City newsboy from the slums. He was in a batch of slum boys sent into the country for two weeks by a charitable foundation.

He found himself, at the end of the journey, in a large, comfortable farmhouse. A motherly woman received him cordially. When bedtime came she took him to a bedroom.

She talked to him, as she turned down the bed covers. This had been her own son's room when he was a boy, she explained. She hoped he would enjoy a good sleep, and be down early in the morning, and so she bade him goodnight.

Morning came and breakfast but the boy didn't appear. She called up the stairs but there was no response.

She went upstairs, found the room door open, and looked in. But there was no boy to be seen. Where was he?

Perplexed and wondering, her eye caught sight of a ragged shoe on the floor at the edge of the bed. Stooping down she saw the boy sound asleep on the floor under the bed.

She called to him: "Time to get up, my boy, breakfast's ready." He came crawling out, rubbing his eyes, "Yes'm, yes'm."

As she turned to leave she said quietly pointing to the bed, "Why didn't you sleep in the bed?"

The boy turned a surprised look, following the line of her pointing finger, toward the bed. "Bed!" he said simply. "Is that a bed?"

He had never slept in a bed. A doorstoop, a box, a barrel, or the like, had been the only bed the boy had ever known.

Are you sleeping under the bed, taking less than Christ has provided?

EIGHT

The Devil's Healing: Imitations and Counterfeits

It is Christ's first will for us that we should be pure in heart, strong in purpose, quick and accurate in discerning evil under any disguise, poised and mature in judgment, gentle in our contacts, content in circumstances, and healed of all our bodily ills and ailments, according to his word, through glad surrender of habit and life to his Spirit's touch.

The Devil: the Ape of God

God is love. The Devil is hate. Love is good, the best good. Hate is evil, the worst evil. The two are sworn enemies. The conflict is utterly irreconcilable. There can be no patched-up truce. It's an advantage to get that fact clear. Neither side will yield. The Devil won't give in. He is incorrigible.

God can't give in. His purity, his character, forbid it. The warfare goes on ceaselessly, but not interminably. There will be an end to it some day, a blessed end, for us. The earth is the battlefield. We are the ones being fought over. Our choice, freely given, is the one thing aimed at in the fighting.

God wants our love, that is, ourselves at our true native best. He wants our love freely, voluntarily given. Love isn't love unless it's freely given.

The Devil wants man's worship, his submission, abject, absolute submission, no matter how it is given or gotten. And he's dead-set on getting it. The Devil is always on the heels of God to hurt man. He will use anything to accomplish that end. Nothing is too base or foul, too refined or cultured, for his reaching hand.

The rarest scholarship and finest culture, the foulest sensuality and most heartless selfishness, each is used to the utmost. Anything to fool and pervert, to get twists and quirks, to lead away from that touch with God that is native to the God-made man.

Nothing is too sacred for the Devil's touch. Christian phraseology, scholastic philosophy, scientific research, are all laid under tribute. The sweetest relationships and purest contacts of life are fully besmirched. And nothing is too foul if it will help his incorrigible purpose. No combination of the sacred and the foul is left untried and unused.

But God is ever on the heels of the Devil to help us. That's why Christ came and died as he did. Nothing God has is too precious to be freely given and sacrificed if only man may be saved from the foul touch of the Devil.

The Devil is an imitator. He's a skilled artful imitator. He never originates. But he has great ability as an imitator. One of the early Christian leaders called the Devil "the ape of God." Imitation is the outstanding trait of both the ape and the Devil. But that was said long ago, long before the leaders' visions had become so obscured.

The Devil doesn't hesitate to deceive. He is dishonest, the father of all sorts of lies. He even slanders God. The Devil is bold, devilishly bold, in his imitations and deceptions. He even imitates God! He steals phraseology from God's Book. He copies God's actions, that is, as nearly as he can.

The expert instantly detects the imitation, the counterfeit, when put side by side with the genuine. But experts in this line are few.

The thing most lacking in Christian circles is teaching, simple, clear, balanced teaching. Characteristically, Christian groups are untaught and untrained. They are like shepherdless sheep, torn, distressed, confused, heading this way and that, running into each other, violently sometimes. It's a marked feature of the spirit conflict.

The great steadying factor is that the outcome is as assured as the fact that Christ emptied that new-hewn tomb of rock, when its purpose had been served.

Miracles appeal to the imagination as nothing else. Any evidence or suggestion of supernatural power in action attracts the biggest crowds in the shortest time. This has always been true, and still is.

It has always been popularly supposed that the supernatural is God at work. A miracle is commonly taken as evidence of divine power. This is a universal common notion or delusion, and has always been so. Of course, intelligent, thoughtful, Christians know that this is not so. Archbishop Trench, the eminent Irish scholar and saint, speaks of this in his notable work on miracles.

A miracle is not necessarily evidence of God's work. It is evidence merely that some supernatural power is in action.

Then the question arises: whose and what? There are two sources of supernatural power: God and the Devil. Of course, God's power is absolute and limitless.

The Devil is distinctly limited. His power is actually much less than sometimes supposed. Still, there is a supernatural power there, however limited. And he is very skillful in using and displaying it to the best advantage.

We are an unsophisticated lot. Worse than that, we are apt to think that we know everything. We prefer to think so.

What a spectacle! We are ignorant, yet we think we know! A mixture of a little knowledge, much ignorance, and more contentment with ourselves just as we are. That's the hardest kind of people to help. That unseen fighter is surely a cunning strategist.

The Bible sheds clear light on every serious question. It will answer, and answer fully, any thoughtful question brought to it. It gives light on this topic. It tells about satanic miracles. A miracle, you will remember, is the result of some power in action greater than men are familiar with. It does not mean something contrary to nature, but something more than the natural thing we are commonly used to.

The Devil's Miracles in Egypt

The Bible tells distinctly about the Devil's miracles. It contains two groups of passages, one past and one regarding the future: Egypt in the past, and the earth-wide crisis that is yet in the future.

In the case of Egypt, it is a time of partial visitation of judgment on the world-empire of the day. Moses performed ten miracles, by God's direction, which vitally affected the nation. The Egyptian magicians, or occult experts, performed three miracles in imitation of Moses, and attempted a fourth, but failed in it. With awe-stricken faces, they admitted that there was a power at work through Moses superior to theirs.

The line of conflict here is sharply drawn. Moses acted by God's direction. The Egyptian king opposed him contemptuously, then stubbornly, then incorrigibly.

The magicians were the king's servants. They were experts in the occult, in dealing with unseen spirits and spiritual forces. They were loyal to Pharaoh in resisting and scoffing at God. They fought Moses and God, with all the power at their command.

The line of conflict is clearly marked. The Devil was opposing God through Pharaoh and his magicians. God and the Devil were the real spiritual opponents behind the human scenes.

It is striking that Pharaoh's magicians performed three miracles through the Devil's power, but failed in performing the fourth.

There is further the tacit inference of a limit in the Devil's power even in the three miracles actually performed.

The magicians caused their rods to become serpents. Perhaps serpent activity was more easily within the Devil's range of action. Yet Moses' serpent swallows up the others! Moses understood that word spoken long after about treading upon serpents.

The turning of water into blood and the plague of countless frogs by the magicians, following Moses' initiative, again reveal the Devil's supernatural power at work.

But again the Devil's power is limited. Moses' miracles suggest an overflowing supply of power. The Devil's is less. The magicians perform the work, yet, there is no flush of power at command, rather a scantiness.

The fourth attempt was a confessed failure. The experts confessed themselves helpless in the face of God's power. They are outdone, outclassed. A little later the magicians themselves were helpless sufferers when the plague of boils came.

The purpose of these satanic miracles is fourfold: to fight God, to discredit his messenger Moses, to deceive the Egyptians and indeed all the world (for such events would travel like wildfire), and to keep God's nation in slavery. It is clearly the Devil at work, behind Pharaoh who is his willing tool.

The limits to the Devil's supernatural power are threefold. The miracles done are imitations of those done through Moses. Each displays less power than the miracle it imitates. And there is a sharp line beyond which the Devil's power cannot go.

It is important to remember, though, that the Devil can work miracles. He has supernatural power, but with sharp, definite limitation.

The Devil's Healings in the Coming Crisis

At the end of the Bible, a time of worldwide crisis that precedes a new order of earthly life is spoken of. It will be a time of marked satanic activity. In connection with it, the Devil will perform miracles of healing. His purpose, of course, is to deceive, to drive through his own plans, and to tighten his hold on people's lives. Let us look at scripture's teaching regarding this.

The common phrase in the New Testament for miracles is the phrase "signs and wonders." Sometimes the language used is "signs," sometimes "signs and wonders," sometimes "signs and wonders and powers," sometimes "signs and powers." A few times the word "miracles" is used.

The greatest number of miracles spoken of are miracles of bodily healing. Of the thirty-three miracles done by Christ twenty-four are miracles of bodily healing. Four others have to do with bodily need.

In the Book of Acts the use of this phrase for miracles of healing is yet more marked. Practically, the phrase "signs and wonders," with its variations, is equivalent in the New Testament to miracles of bodily healing. Other usage is so exceptional as to emphasize this as the common rule.

Notice that this is the phrase used for a distinctive phase of satanic activity during that coming crisis. There are three outstanding passages: in the Gospels, in the writings of Paul, and in the Book of Revelation.

In his Olivet talk with four disciples, less than a week before his crucifixion, Christ speaks of the crisis preceding his own coming and the new order of life.

He speaks of various characteristics of that tribulation-crisis. He says, "There shall arise false Christs (evil men pretending to be Christ), and false prophets (or religious teachers), and shall show *great signs and wonders.*"

Then he says that the works will be directed against Christ's followers. It is "to lead astray, if (that be) possible, even the elect," *i.e.,* Christ's own people (Mt 24:24, Mk 13:22).

Taking the phrase "signs and wonders" at its common meaning in the New Testament, this would mean, to the four disciples listening, that there will be marked miracles of healing by satanic power, during that climax of evil, for the express purpose of deceiving and leading astray Christ's own people.

In his second letter to the disciples at Thessalonica, Paul is answering some questions that have arisen about just when Christ's return was to be expected. He explains that there will be a great evil leader in action, around whom the coming Crisis will center.

This leader will be at the very height of his blasphemous career at the time of Christ's coming. He will be destroyed by the glorious appearance of Christ (the blazing forth or shining forth of his arrival).

Then Paul speaks of the marked traits of this evil leader, the Antichrist, this personification of the Devil. His activity will be "according to the working of Satan with all *power and signs and wonders of falsehood,*" or "lying wonders." That is, these miracles are done in imitation of Christ's miracles, to deceive the people and lead them astray (2 Thes 2:9, 10).

Here is the same phrase again. Paul's use of it would mean only one thing to these Thessalonian disciples: miracles of healing by satanic power to deceive.

A parallel passage is found in one of Moses' talks given at the Plains of Moab (Dt 13:1-3). He is speaking of what is to be done if a false prophet certifies his message by "a sign or a wonder," so as to lead the people away from the true worship. Plainly, miraculous deception was quite familiar to the Israelites.

The Book of Revelation message is the same. It is spoken of repeatedly as one of the marked characteristics of the campaign of deception in that brief, terrific, future crisis.

John describes the activity of an evil leader who will be the immediate associate of that foul Antichrist (Rv 13:13-14). He is a religious leader, a sort of court-preacher to the Antichrist himself, who reigns as a king of kings for a brief time.

Among other things, this stands out in the description, "and he doeth *great signs* that he should even make fire to come down out of heaven upon the earth in the sight of men. And he deceiveth them that dwell on the earth by reason of *the signs*."

The startling action of fire coming down is specified in speaking of the great signs. This stands out in addition to the usual meaning of the phrase "great signs."

A little later, John is told of happenings toward the end of that crisis period. Sent out by the Devil himself and by his two chief leaders, the Antichrist and his court-preacher, will be "spirits of demons *working signs*" (Rv 16:13-14).

In speaking of the utter defeat and rout of the Antichrist and his evil associates, this court-preacher or religious teacher, is identified as the one "that wrought the signs . . . wherewith he deceived them." Clearly, these *signs* are an outstanding feature (Rv 19:19, 20). This emphasis of a fivefold repetition is striking.

The whole New Testament use of the phrase makes clear that miracles of healing by satanic power will be one of the most common, if not the most common, feature of that crisis time that is coming. The purpose is to deceive the people, particularly the church constituency. It is to make them think that God is at work. Uninstructed as they so largely are, and not keen to discern, they will be easy prey to these tactics.

The Devil's Healing Today

One need not go back to Egypt, nor forward to the coming crisis time. We can find references to Satan's works close at hand. Our own time is witnessing this sort of thing in marked measure and increasing extent.

The church of Christ has not been true to the full Gospel of Christ. I say that very thoughtfully and sadly. I do not say it to criticize the church, but only to help understand things at the present time.

I love the church. I reverence its past, and its present inestimable service in the world. If my words seem critical, I am simply criticizing myself, so far as any man is a part of the church.

With fine exceptions, the church of Christ has not told fully in any generation, since the first few Christian centuries, the full, rounded Gospel of Christ. So it is not surprising that false teachings about bodily healing have grown up. The great need for healing everywhere has created a rare opportunity to teach about bodily healing in a wrong way. The people are hungry, eager for help. And the Devil is never slow in using every open door, or every door that he could pry open.

Just now there is a system of teaching about healing, and a system of healing that has gained popularity. It has spread like a wildfire in our own land, up and down Europe, into Africa and the Orient, and, indeed, wherever the Anglo-American trail leaves traces.

It uses Christ's name quite freely. It quotes or rather half-quotes and misquotes, the Bible. Its teaching is a mixture of Christian phraseology, devout language, psychological half-truths, and positive untruths.

It makes pretense of being a Chistian church. I need not repeat its name, it is so well known.* The thing to notice is that people are healed through its ministrations, within sharply marked limitations and restrictions.

Remember what was said in a previous chapter on the seven ways in which healing comes to one's body. The Creator has graciously put a healing power within the human body. It is natural healing with conscious cooperation on our part.

Our mental attitude is often the decisive thing in illness, turning the tide in favor of healing and

---

*It is thought that the author is referring to the religion known as Christian Science.

health. Enlightened, instructed understanding of this remarkable healing power in the body, and our intelligent cooperation, make an enormous difference. This is the second way in which healing comes. It should be noted. It will be spoken of again later.

Another form of healing is accomplished through this same natural power assisted by human wisdom and skill, both personal and professional. Still further, this natural power sometimes *overcomes* what was done by blundering, unwise human touch. These are the four natural ways.

The two supernatural ways of healing include Christ's direct touch in addition to the creative natural power, and the Devil's touch. The seventh way healing may come is through the blending of two or more of these.

There are seven ways in which healing may come to one's body: four natural, two supernatural, and one a blend or combination of two or more of these. In this false system we are talking about, this so-called Christian system, the healings that do occur come through two of these ways.

Much emphasis is put on the second of these, the human understanding of, and cooperation with, that natural healing power. I do not mean to say that it is taught in a clear, intelligent fashion. Clear teaching is conspicuously absent here. A strange garbled mixture of truths and half-truths and untruths are taught. But through it all is a continual emphasis on one's mental attitude.

So far as this insistence actually affects one's attitude that inner power of healing swings into action. This is good so far as healing is good.

If the teaching were clear, and more, if it were put in right connection with other teaching that belongs with it, the results would be yet better. But, of course, this teaching is unclear and incomplete.

No evil system of teaching is all bad. It would fall of its own dead weight. The Devil always steals a veneer of truth for his lies. He is the first expert in the fine art of camouflage.

The truth about the influence of the mind on the body, so little appreciated to the full by any one, was true for Adam and Eve in Eden, for Cain outside Eden, with the wickedest man that ever lived as with the saintliest, in savage wilds as in cultured centers.

God's creative touch is never off anyone's body. This is one of the seven ways of healing emphasized partly by this false system of healing.

There is a second way used in this false teaching. It highlights a strange fact. *The Devil heals* through this so-called Christian teaching.

"Why," you instantly cry out, "the Devil heal! Absurd! Ridiculous! The Devil is bad. Healing is only good. Will a bad Devil do a good thing?"

The answer is that a bad Devil will do a good thing for a bad purpose, to get hold on a person's life and to tighten his hold.

Imagine that a mongrel dog back of your house disturbs your evening's sleep, night after night. You are too gentle-hearted to use a revolver. So you get a bit of good meat and some bad poison. You combine them dexterously. You throw the mixture in the back alley.

The dog has no sense of discernment between good meat and bad poison. He eats the good meat greedily. He gets the bad poison. The city's garbage cart has an extra job. And now your night's slumbers are undisturbed. The strategy was a success.

Some good people, even some Christians, might claim close kinship with that dog in one particular. They have no discernment, no spiritual discernment. They are easily caught in the false teaching with the Christian phraseology, but don't detect the absence of truthful teaching or the actual presence of the Devil's own teachings.

Christ's Blood: the Touchstone

Spirit discernment is one of the rarest, if not the rarest thing today. This is true even in cultured Christian circles. It is strangely true how lacking discernment is.

The outstanding characteristic of preaching today is the bewitching, bewildering mixture and blend of half-truths, nontruths, and the absence of the few essential truths. The whole is covered with a more or less highly polished veneer of religious talk or Christian verbiage. Pleasing personality, vigorous mentality, fine diction, scholarly quotations and allusions—all cloud the real message being given.

This is true in all of Christendom, including the mission lands, with some exceptions.

How can we know what teaching to accept about bodily healing? We all work busily trying to make ends meet. We can't all be experts. How shall we know?

The answer is simple. A single ray of clear shining sun will pierce right through the fogs that gather. There is a touchstone by which to test any teaching, whether in type or on tongue. It's an acid test, unfailing.

It is the singular personality of Christ and the distinctive solitary meaning of his death on Calvary and his living again afterward.

Supernatural healing should be accepted only where the deity of Christ is distinctly emphasized, and the sacrificial blood he shed for us, as none other did nor could nor can, is made blessedly prominent.

The Devil hates the blood of the solitary God-Man. He fears it. He crouches terrified and flees where it is emphasized and pled in prayer. The blood spells out his stinging defeat. And he knows it.

Two things should be keenly noted about the Devil's healing. There is a distinct line beyond which he cannot go. Over that line he is powerless. Christ healed perfectly, permanently, and instantly, and he still does when we allow it. The Devil's healings are never perfect nor permanent.

One remembers the Egyptian story. There the Devil's supernatural power was limited. In comparison with God it was scanty and brought about minor results. It was in imitation always, mere imitation.

The second thing to notice is that *the Devil's healing makes slaves*. It leads to a bondage of spirit, of mental vigor, and a moral bondage that has a viselike grip.

This slavery can be broken only through the power of the blood of Christ, and then, usually, only through the most severe mental and spiritual struggle. But it can be broken. Christ's blood will set anyone blessedly free. Anyone, anytime, who will come to Christ, trusting as simply as a little child and as fully as the maturest adult.

With all perplexities and burdens, one may come. And Christ never fails. His blood cleanses from sin. It breaks the Devil's shackles. And it heals our bodies.

The Power of the Blood of Christ

One winter my wife and I met a German deaconess in Stockholm, who told us an unusual story. She was a woman in middle life, of large frame and full of physical vigor. She had been engaged for years in mission work in Berlin, especially among girls and young women.

We were guests together in the same home for a week, and had many opportunities for fellowship and exchange of experiences. We came to respect her for her common sense and cautious mature judgments, and to love her for her evident saintliness and her sacrificial life in the difficult field of service into which she had been led.

The incident she recounted to us was one of many. I would hesitate to tell it were it not for the sanity, and cautiousness, and thoughtful care in detailed observation, that marked her speech. As I listened and questioned and thought and prayed throughout that week, I found an answer of acceptance in my inner spirit to her unusual story.

The story concerned a woman whom she knew personally who lived out in the country not far from Berlin. Her little daughter accidentally fell into an open fire and was seriously burned on her face.

The woman did a thing that seems incredible. She went out to an old tree in the forest, and there made a pact with the Devil, that if he would heal her daughter of the burn she would serve him faithfully.

The thing seemed impossible, both in terms of the willingness to do such a thing, and that such a transaction could take place. But the woman herself, afterward, told the story to the deaconess who was telling us. And it was clearly real to the woman who said she made the pact.

The woman said that at once her child's face looked as if the fire had not touched it. The healing seemed complete. No scars remained. That's the first part of the story. The child grew to be a beautiful young woman. Meanwhile, they had moved in to Berlin and settled there. The young woman attended some meetings at a mission hall and was deeply impressed. One night she accepted Christ as her personal Savior and dedicated her life to him. I think the mother herself had become a Christian about this same time.

At once, the marks of the fire appeared on her daughter's face as though just fresh. The deaconess was present. They were all greatly distressed. The mother explained to the deaconess about the earlier experience.

The deaconess knew about Christ's healing power, and taught the mother and daughter about it. They had a time of prayer together. The deaconess told us Christ's healing touch came.

And again the young woman's face showed no marks of the fire. The deaconess herself witnessed this.

The story is the more striking in telling of a double healing, the Devil's and Christ's. It illustrates the very real rivalry between the two; bitter and hopeless on the Devil's side, insistent and certain of victory on Christ's side.

The human will, sovereign in its choice, decides in that conflict. Here was a decisive defeat for the Devil and the sweeping victory of Christ on the battlefield of one human life. The young woman's decision, insisted on under stress, was the decisive factor.

The Devil's intense selfishness stands out, his spiteful spirit. He touches only to hurt. He helps only to help himself. The Devil is always on the heels of God to hurt. God is ever quick as a flash on the heels of the Devil to reach eagerly out and help and heal.

Christ was God himself coming down to the battlefield. He gave the Devil the decisive blow. And so we may be set free. We are made strong to choose right, and only right, regardless of consequences.

The School of Discernment

A great need today among Christian people is *spiritual discernment,* though not the critical spirit that hunts heresies and picks flaws. That only hurts the hunter and helps no one. Nagging criticism is like a sharp-edged knife that has no hilt. It cuts the hand that uses it.

Discernment means the trained ear that listens attentively and discerns the main point of a teaching, under whatever rhetorical veneer. It means the opened eye quick to see between the lines what is really there, maybe in hiding. It means the humble spirit, willing to see its own faults and defects, only eager to be right. It means the loving spirit quick to give any help to any man.

The sore need today is for teaching, not argument and discussion, but teaching. Never was the need greater. Argument only hardens. Teaching, the clear, positive, patient teaching of God's truth, put into the sort of language men speak, with simple illustrations out of real life, this is sorely needed.

One should cultivate an accurate discernment or appraisal of all that meets eye and ear. We should do it for self-protection, and for true culture, and to help others.

There's a school of discernment. We ought to take time for this special course. The requirements for entrance are few and simple. They are five in number: an act, a habit, a book, a bit of time, and a spirit.

The act? surrender to Christ as the Master. The

habit? doing habitually what would please him in everything. And when in doubt, *don't*. The Book? this rare, singularly, solitary Book of God. The time? the daily bit of quiet time alone with the Bible, with the mind alert, and the spirit open. The spirit? the spirit of prayer for understanding, discernment, seeing things as they are. With this is the thoughtful, reflective spirit.

With all of these goes the willing spirit, willingness to accept facts and conclusions that you don't like, that run contrary to your pre-conceptions and preferences and habits.

If we will only start in this school and attend faithfully, it will be of the rarest value in the coming days, the coming difficult days. The outcome will be mental and spiritual discern-ment, a keen and growing discernment. With it will grow the brotherly spirit that will help any one in personal need no matter how he differs from you, or criticizes you.

Whoever is willing to do Christ's will for him, regardless of how it may affect personal aspir-ations, will have in increasing degree that keen, clear knowledge of truth, of the Book's teaching, of Christ himself who embodies all truth in himself (Jn 7:17).

The clear vision, the discriminating ear, the balanced understanding of things that differ, the obedient spirit, the heart of love in all one's personal contacts, these are some results of attendance at the school of discernment.

Whether in school or out, there is healing for our bodies through the solitary God-Man who died as none other did nor could nor can, and lived again, and still lives. Through this Man's blood comes deliverance from any bondage full, sweet, glad, free deliverance.

Christ waits at your side now.

Also from Servant Publications

The Open Secret
Hannah Whitall Smith

The Bible contains a secret—the secret of how to love God and follow him in living a joy-filled and fruitful life. You will find no better key to that secret than the writings of Hannah Whitall Smith, known to millions as the author of *The Christian's Secret of a Happy Life*. *The Open Secret* is a classic devotional that speaks graciously of the love of God, of his forgiveness, his patience, and his call to men and women to know him personally. *$5.95*